Serial Killers and the Phenomenon of Serial Murder

A Student Textbook

David Wilson, Elizabeth Yardley and Adam Lynes

With a Foreword by Steve Hall

WATERSIDE PRESS

ial Killers and the Phenomenon of Serial Murder

Student Textbook

avid Wilson, Elizabeth Yardley and Adam Lynes

ISBN 978-1-914603-07-5
ISBN 978-1-906534-25-7 (Epub e-book)
ISBN 978-1-906534-34-9 (Adobe e-book)

Cataloguing-In-Publication Data A catalogue record for this book can be obtained on request from the British Library.

UK distributor Gardners Books, 1 Whittle Drive, Eastbourne, East Sussex, BN23 6QH. Tel: +44 (0)1323 521777; sales@gardners.com; www.gardners.com

North American distributor Ingram Book Company, One Ingram Blvd, La Vergne, TN 37086, USA. Tel: (+1) 615 793 5000; inquiry@ingramcontent.com

Printed by CPI Antony Rowe, Chippenham, Wiltshire.

e-book *Serial Killers and the Phenomenon of Serial Murder* is available as an ebook and also to subscribers of Myilibrary, Dawsonera, ebrary, EBL and Ebscohost.

Published 2015 by
Waterside Press
Sherfield Gables
Sherfield on Loddon
Hook, Hampshire
United Kingdom RG27 0JG

Telephone +44(0)1256 882250
E-mail enquiries@watersidepress.co.uk
Online catalogue WatersidePress.co.uk

CONTENTS

ABOUT THE AUTHORS

Professor David Wilson is one of the UK's leading criminologists, a National Teaching Fellow and presenter of a number of crime-related TV programmes. Based at Birmingham City University where he is Founding Director of the Centre for Applied Criminology, his books for Waterside Press include *Serial Killers: Hunting Britons and Their Victims 1960-2006* (2007) and *Mary Ann Cotton: Britain's First Female Serial Killer* (2013).

Dr Elizabeth Yardley is a Reader in Criminology and Director of the Centre for Applied Criminology at Birmingham City University. Her research focuses upon homicide and violent crime with a particular emphasis upon female serial killers and the role of digital communication media in homicide. Her publications include the *Female Serial Killers in Social Context* (2015 forthcoming, Policy Press) and the 'Making Sense of Facebook Murder? Social Networking Sites and Contemporary Homicide' (*Howard Journal*, 2015), the first piece of research to explore the role of social networking sites in homicide.

Adam Lynes is a Lecturer in Criminology at Birmingham City University and Deputy Head of the Homicide and Violent Crime (HaVoC) research cluster within the Centre for Applied Criminology. His research predominantly focuses on the significance of occupational choice for serial murderers and his publications include 'Driving, Pseudo-Reality and the BTK: A Case Study' (2015 forthcoming, *Journal of Forensic Psychology and Offender Profiling*, with David Wilson) and, drawing upon his degree in English Literature, 'Zola and the Serial Killer: Robert Black and La Bête Humaine' (Lynes *et al*, 2012, *International Journal of Criminology and Sociology*). He has also studied and written about other forms of violent crime, including the act of family annihilation, in 'A Taxonomy of Male British Family Annihilators, 1980–2012' (2014, Yardley *et al*, *Howard Journal*).

ACKNOWLEDGEMENTS

The authors would like to thank Steve Hall for his warm words of encouragement; the librarians of a number of university libraries, especially of Birmingham City University and Cambridge University Library; everyone at Waterside Press; and our undergraduate and postgraduate students who have shaped our thinking about serial killers and the phenomenon of serial murder.

David Wilson would particularly like to thank Barbara McCalla and the peerless Bryan Gibson.

Elizabeth Yardley would particularly like to thank the PhD students in the Centre for Applied Criminology, whose interest in and enthusiasm for our work always drives our research forward.

Adam Lynes would especially like to thank his family for all their love, support, and encouragement. In particular for his parents who taught him the value of critical understanding and supported him in all his academic pursuits, and his grandmother, Brenda, whose love and support helped make his dreams and aspirations a reality.

THE AUTHOR OF THE FOREWORD

Steve Hall is Professor of Criminology at Teesside University and the co-founder of the Teesside Centre for Realist Criminology. He is an internationally leading criminological researcher and theorist. His book *Theorizing Crime and Deviance* (Sage 2012) was lauded as 'a remarkable intellectual achievement' that 'rocks the foundations of the discipline'.

FOREWORD

When I taught big core criminological theory modules to undergraduates I was often confronted with the fascination many students have for serial killing. They want to know why a small number of people do such horrific things to each other. The easiest way out of that particular challenge is to dismiss the whole issue as voyeuristic, sensationalist and too rare to be of significance, the stuff of vacuous 'true crime' magazines and therefore unworthy of the attention of a sophisticated discipline such as criminology. The criminological establishment issued stern warnings: to sensationalise extreme behaviour is to demonise individuals, or to misrepresent humanity by unduly emphasising its extremes and offering unwelcome support to the old conservative position that something wicked lies at the core of the human condition. In a post-war criminological paradigm that grew out of a critical stance towards labelling and authoritarian governance, some criminologists were convinced that to focus on serial killing was distasteful, politically dangerous and a distraction from the task of addressing the real issues, which of course should be the defence of individual criminals as victimised actors and the critique of the crimes of the powerful and their corporate states.

Maintaining such a pious position was not easy because, of course, the students' curiosity was always more powerful than critical criminology's attempts to deflect it onto something that was considered more politically wholesome. They kept on asking. At the time serial killing was not my specialism but I decided against such evasive piety and took up the challenge of tracking down sophisticated theoretical frameworks that could go some way to explaining the phenomenon. I discovered that some excellent work was available on the social psychology and cultural contexts of serial killing. This work dug a lot deeper than the medico-psychological and biological determinist models that held sway in some schools of psychology. A small number of theorists related the phenomenon to the destructive norms and drives at the core of military-industrial societies, but this fascinating work has been marginalised by mainstream criminology and critical criminology alike. Students often discovered that it was wrapped up in very complex psychoanalytical terms that required a firmer grounding in that particular discipline than most of them had been given.

I realised that I had made a pragmatic decision based on the same grounds that justify those who argue for public criminology. If the students' curiosity in this area was not to be deflected it was better to point them towards analyses that are far more serious and responsible than those they might find in the popular media or conservative criminology. So it was during my search for sophisticated yet undergraduate-friendly studies of serial killing—which for me had to be more erudite than deterministic medico-psychological models yet braver and more explanatory than social constructionist evasions—that I came upon David Wilson's earlier work on the subject. Of course Wilson has been a high-profile public criminologist for some time and I have always admired the way he combines populism with intellectual responsibility. As a former prison governor he has also benefitted from face-to-face experience with serial killers and is acutely aware that their accounts of their own motivations were usually unreliable. It took someone with great honesty and open-mindedness to realise that if the killers themselves don't know precisely why they committed such brutal crimes it might, for the time being at least, remain a mystery for the rest of us.

What Wilson did with this thorny and controversial subject was a revelation to myself and my students. In his book *Serial Killers: Hunting Britons and Their Victims* (Waterside Press, 2007) he managed to produce an exemplary analysis of serial killing that acknowledged some of the more convincing psychological and cultural explanations yet placed the phenomenon fully in its social and economic contexts—and all this in a clear and unpretentious style that the students lapped up. It was these contexts that made this such an unusually clear and powerful analysis as it connected the study of serial killing and the serial killer to important sociological and political analyses of the times in which we live.

In this new book, written with colleagues Elizabeth Yardley and Adam Lynes, Wilson has gone one better to produce a student-friendly and practitioner-friendly primer that lays out the whole issue and its underlying contexts in a very clear and comprehensive text. The French social thinker Jean Baudrillard once said that we have entered the era of 'extreme phenomena'. Extreme behaviour has become the normal punctuation in the course of everyday life. In everyday life outside military conflict little is more extreme than serial killing in terms of the uncontrollable power of human drives and the harm their acting out can inflict on other human beings. It defies standard explanations of rational choice, social strain or mental illness to present itself as an example of what Jacques Lacan called 'the Real', the inexplicable aspect of reality that irrupts on our senses and leaves a trace that we cannot understand. Understanding such real things out there in what the new speculative realist philosophers are calling 'the great outdoors' is supposed to be the criminologist's job—something that has been lost in the era of social constructionism. However Wilson and his team warn us of the crude positivism and determinism of the 'medico-psychological' model. Individual motivations are often so complex and variegated as to be inexplicable, therefore it is important to examine with great care the structural context in which serial murder occurs.

The framework deployed in this book moves beyond biology and psychology—whilst not ignoring their insights—to construct a contextualised victim-centred structural analysis of vulnerability. It shows how perpetrator-victim relations tend to be aligned with social power relations, class and patriarchy whilst avoiding the dogma that can often be associated with such positions. More importantly, the argument is threaded together with an underlying historical analysis that shows a decline in serial killing in the inter-war years of collective spirit, socioeconomic inclusion and care–a cultural climate in which people mattered to each other. Whilst this might been seen by some as a nostalgic yearning that flies in the face of popular and academic arguments that we are living in progressive emancipatory times, the low frequency of serial killing combines with other low rates of social problems in that period to give the argument an empirical credibility that is difficult to ignore. Greater socioeconomic stability than we have in the current neoliberal era means fewer family and community breakdowns, and fewer vulnerable victims such as runaway children or sex workers operating in unguarded locales that are easy targets for perpetrators. From this broader and deeper perspective we can learn more about victims, perpetrators and their psychosocial relations. For this reason alone, the book is an important introduction for students looking for a responsible social scientific approach to a phenomenon that is so susceptible to popular sensationalism and academic reductionism alike.

The book moves on to introduce other important aspects of the phenomenon, such as the difficulty of pinning down the female serial killer, often a bewildering combination of occupational, hearthside and instrumental/expressive types that does not fit formulaic explanations or operate in standard contexts. The authors also challenge mainstream criminological theories of representation by showing in fine detail how the standard media studies conception of serial killing as a prime example of sensationalism and newsworthiness needs to be more finely honed: some serial killers are ignored, therefore it is not simply the individualised 'horror' of their actions that helps the media sell their stories.

The argument in this book does not preach from any typical standpoint position, although it acknowledges insights from such positions and leaves them open to debate. It introduces students to empirical complexity and avoids dogma. It's not too heavy on theory, which for a primer is probably a wise move, but it offers students a gentle introduction that poses important questions as it hits the ball into their court. It does not close the students' minds in the reductionist way that some standpoint positions do but opens them in a way that will encourage further reading and independent and progressive thought about one of the most disturbing and impenetrable of all criminological issues.

Steve Hall
May 2015

INTRODUCTION

The description "serial killer" has the power to fascinate and attract, as much as it shocks, repels and disgusts. We want to know more about the people whom we label in this way because they seem to operate outside of our moral universe—something which can be both frightening and exciting all at the same time.

So, it was perhaps no surprise when Joanne Dennehy from Peterborough in Cambridgeshire, admitted at the Old Bailey in London in November 2013 to killing three men earlier in that year that she attracted a storm of media attention. Dennehy—who has a distinctive facial tattoo—admitted in court to killing her landlord, Kevin Lee, and her two housemates, Lukasz Slaboszewski and John Chapman, seemingly stabbing them all and then dumping their bodies in a ditch. A number of newspapers quickly described her as a "serial killer", which only seemed to increase the media's interest in her case.[1]

But was she really a serial killer by any accepted, academic definition of the term, or was she instead a murderer, a multiple murderer or perhaps even a spree killer? Does it in fact matter how we label Dennehy given how unusual her crimes are, especially in Britain?

There will be some who will claim that this is an interesting but "academic point" (by which there is an implication that it is not important at all) and, while we accept which label to apply might at first seem to be of little practical value, in fact it matters a great deal—something which we discuss in detail in *Chapter One*. Indeed this academic textbook has been written to introduce students to the reality of the phenomenon of serial murder and what it is that we mean when we label someone as a serial killer, rather than the froth, mystique and fantasy that has developed around these subjects.

1. Joanne Dennehy is frequently and incorrectly referred to as Joanna by the press and online.

It does this by introducing students to the various academic controversies that surround these topics, as well as deconstructing a number of more popular myths. It largely concentrates on British cases—both recent and historical—and looks at a range of scholarly and more popular issues that are regularly discussed when cases such as Dennehy's are described in the press, by law enforcement, or by Criminologists. As such, a number of case studies are presented in *Chapters Three, Six* and *Eight*. These are used to bring the theoretical materials that we offer to life and also to remind students that Criminology is an applied as well as a theoretical discipline. Indeed we will use Dennehy throughout the remainder of this *Introduction* to illustrate a number of the themes which will re-appear within the text and which will get you to start thinking more critically about the phenomenon of serial murder and why you should be interested in serial killers.

Themes and Issues

One such theme is to consider just exactly why we—and especially you—are so fascinated by serial killers. Do you see yourself like the fictional Clarice Starling interviewing the serial killing psychiatrist Dr Hannibal Lector in the novel *The Silence of the Lambs*? Or perhaps you are intrigued by what is known as "offender profiling" and want one day to become a profiler for the police? Perhaps you are curious about the various typologies that have been developed about serial killers. Indeed, we know that all of these influences are why a number of our students decided to study Criminology and then to choose a module, or option that deals with this subject. But more broadly, what is it about the gruesome crimes committed about serial killers that grips your imagination? We know that what they do is appalling but, somehow, we don't want to—metaphorically—look away from what it is that they have done. In other words, and to return to one of our earlier questions, just exactly why was there a media storm about Dennehy?

Clearly there is going to be more than one answer to this particular question—and several others are presented in the chapters that follow—but most immediately we might want to remember that when we consider serial killers from an academic perspective there is a safe boundary between us and the serial killers that we are studying. In other words, there is something which we might call "a protective frame" between us and our interest in serial killers so that any real danger is in fact minimised or, more bluntly, non-existent. In this way studying serial killers is like going to watch a horror movie—it is frightening, but we know that it's not "real" and therefore we can enjoy the action on the screen. There is in reality no danger but our fear and enjoyment are all the same and no less diminished. Note these two different emotions—fear and enjoyment. Psychologists describe this ability of people to be able to take pleasure from two different emotions at the same time as "coactivation".

Key Term — Coactivation

Definition: Coactivation is the activation of two or more things together, such as being happy and sad at the same time. Think, for example, about the first time you came to University. You might have been sad to have left your home, family and friends, but also happy about the potential to experience something new.

Of course having to deal with a real serial killer would be a very different experience and, most obviously, there would be no protective frame; the dangers, in other words, would be all too obvious. And, more importantly, that serial killer would have in reality taken the lives of some of our fellow human beings, as opposed to having "killed" actors in a movie, or the characters in a book.

Yet another reason to explain our fascination with serial killers might be that we regard someone who kills repeatedly over time as mysterious and, as humans, we have a deep psychological and in-built need to solve mysteries. Someone who repeatedly kills appears bizarre to us and so we need to explain that behaviour, which in turn allows us to feel that we can control—or at least predict—this behaviour, or when it might occur. Looked at from this perspective, studying serial killers and more broadly the phenomenon of serial murder is therefore a very rational thing to do.

It may indeed be rational to study serial killers but, of course, serial killing is extremely rare and therefore the chances having to deal with an actual case of serial murder is equally unusual. Might not our time therefore as Criminologists be spent to better ends? This is something we consider more fully towards the end of this *Introduction.* But here we might simply note that this rarity seems to only magnify popular attention when such a case—or even a potential case like Dennehy's—emerges and as Criminologists we are often asked to comment on what has happened. What should we say?

This rarity in reality that we have described does not extend to how TV, film, books, and the print and broadcast media use serial murder and serial killers. On TV we can think of Dexter, Red John and Hannibal and series such as *The Fall* and *The Following;* on screen there is *Psycho, The Texas Chainsaw Massacre, American Psycho* and, most famously, *The Silence of the Lambs*; and in print the novels of Val McDermid, Patricia Cornwell, Stieg Larsson and Jo Nesbo. Even so, we have to acknowledge that serial killers appear in fiction or on screen in numbers that are grossly disproportionate to their actual significance. Nesbo, for example, has had his fictional detective Harry Hole capture or track down six serial killers, even if Norway—where these novels are set—has in fact only had to experience one such murderer. To what extent do we consume these fictional serial killers so that they become our understanding of the phenomenon? Perhaps it is celluloid serial killers that we find fascinating, as opposed to real ones? This is an issue which we discuss more fully within *Chapter Nine.*

Of course the academic context in which to discuss serial murder is the reality of violent crime, including murder. However, we need to remember that even the offence which we label as "murder" is a very blunt description which does not really capture the diversity of what we call "murder". How are we to compare, for example, the young man who murders another man in a pub that he thinks has insulted him, with the actions of a mother who kills her child within 24 hours of having given birth? Indeed, we even have a special name for this latter type of unlawful killing—neonaticide—just to show how different it is from the confrontational murders of drunk young men in pubs.

Confrontational murder is the most common that we find in this country—murder is a young man's business, and it is usually young men from lower socio-economic backgrounds killing other young men from similar backgrounds. Of all the murders committed in this country nearly 90 per cent are committed by men, who will usually stab, occasionally shoot, or strangle their friends, and sometimes complete strangers (for an overview of murder in Britain see Brookman, 2005).

Women who murder usually kill within their family—most often their children—and when they kill they will usually smother, poison or strangle, although they also occasionally stab. Women like Theresa Riggi killed her three children in her Edinburgh flat in 2010 from fear that she would lose them in a custody battle. We call women like Riggi "family annihilators".

Key Term — Family Annihilator

Definition: Family annihilators are a type of murderer—usually male—who will take the lives of their child or children, their partner or ex-partner, and then commit suicide, or at least make a serious attempt to do so.

However, this does not seem to have been the context, or the circumstances in which Dennehy came to kill and perhaps it was simply the fact that she was a woman who repeatedly murdered that attracted the media's attention? If that is the case it would seem that there are better examples of women who have murdered to compare her with than the family annihilator Theresa Riggi.

We discuss women like Myra Hindley, Rose West, Beverley Allitt and Mary Ann Cotton—all British serial killers— more fully in *Chapters Seven* and *Eight.* Cotton was our first female serial killer, executed in Durham in 1873 for poisoning her stepson, but who may have murdered as many as 17 people by serving them tea, broth or soup laced with arsenic. As well as her stepson, she probably murdered her mother, a number of her children and step-children, three husbands, a lover and an inconvenient friend. She was a "comfort killer"—in other words she killed because she benefitted both financially and socially from these deaths by inheriting small amounts of cash which in turn allowed her to find other husbands who had more wealth or prestige.

Cotton murdered alone, although often in public, as neighbours, friends and even doctors came to minister to those family members and friends that she was slowly poisoning. On the other hand both Hindley and West murdered with a male partner and they usually murdered strangers to them—victims often chosen by Ian Brady in Hindley's case or by her husband Fred in Rose's. Hindley and West were part of a "killer couple", although why they should want to follow the lead of their partners needs to be considered. We sometimes call female serial killers like Hindley and West "disciples" as they kill because they want praise from their "idol" and are therefore prepared to do anything that he asks. Unlike the "comfort killer" who seems to gain no sexual satisfaction from the fact that she is murdering, the "disciple" is much more fully engaged in the murders that she commits with her partner and can often enjoy the sexual thrill of taking another person's life.

West and Hindley may have been hybristophiliacs—they gained sexual arousal by being with men who were known to be cruel and sadistic and they, in turn, came to enjoy that cruelty and sadism for themselves. They were, or at least became, sexual predators, a type of female serial killer that is exceedingly rare, and even in an American context—the home of serial murder—only Aileen Wuornos might fit this category, although unlike Hindley or West, she operated independently killing men that she picked up whilst working selling sexual services.

One final British serial killer with whom to compare Dennehy is less well-known and it is interesting to note how West and Hindley have emerged into public consciousness while Beverley Allitt has all but disappeared—a subject we discuss more fully in *Chapter Nine*. Even so Allitt was convicted of killing four young children and of attempting to murder three others while she was employed as a nurse at Grantham and Kesteven Hospital in 1991. These murders and the attempted murders all took place within just 59 days. Unlike Hindley and West, Allitt has a mental health problem and has been diagnosed as suffering from Munchausen Syndrome by Proxy. She is now held at Rampton Secure Hospital and perhaps her public disappearance has to do with the fact that with Allitt we know why she killed—she was mentally-ill.

Key Term — Munchausen Syndrome

Definition: Munchausen Syndrome is sometimes known as "Hospital Addiction Syndrome" in which the person feigns illness or trauma to draw attention or sympathy to themselves. If it is "by proxy" the person suffering from this psychiatric condition will abuse another person — most often a child — so as to garner sympathy or attention.

How should we judge Dennehy? Serial killer, family annihilator, comfort killer, disciple, sexual predator or simply as a multiple murderer? For the moment let's just conclude that what she did was exceedingly unusual in our culture and that murder—including multiple and serial murder—remains a man's business.

Why Study Serial Killers?

We contend that understanding and then labelling Dennehy is important because accurately describing this type of killer not only allows us to begin to better appreciate the specific crime being discussed but also more generally helps us to better understand the reality of violent crime, murder and the phenomenon of serial murder more broadly. In turn this assists law enforcement through helping to accurately identify crime patterns and trends in different types of offences and offenders—all crucial in "case linkage", which therefore helps to prevent "linkage blindness".

Key Term—Case Linkage

Definition: Case linkage recognises links between previously unrelated cases through analysing similar or distinctive *modus operandi* (methods of operating) at the crime scene by the perpetrator, such as victim selection and physical evidence.

But does this argument—this justification—not simply perpetuate rather than challenge ways of viewing the phenomenon of serial murder? For example, in seeking to try to "understand" what might have motivated Dennehy to kill in the end we collude with the dominant tradition of writing about serial murderers—which is called the "medico-psychological" tradition. Within this approach, what matters are the biological, genetic, psychological roots of what it might have been that propelled or "determined" the killer to kill. Is this a particularly helpful way of understanding this phenomenon, or does a victim-centred and "structural approach" better answer our questions? This is an issue that is all too rarely discussed within academic and especially popular writing about serial murder, but is something which we consider more fully *Chapter Two*. This structural approach will inform the remainder of the textbook and is something which you should bear in mind as you are reading. After all, as David Wilson has described it—despite having interviewed a number of serial killers –

> "I am simply not interested in any particular serial killer—his background, his relationship with his family and friends, what his school-

> days might have been like, whether he prefers jam to marmalade. Rather I want to understand whom he (it is almost always a 'he') was able to kill." (Wilson, 2009: vii).

It is Wilson's analysis and victim-centred approach of the groups that are targeted by serial killers that informs our overview of British serial killing which we present in *Chapter Four*, although we also use new, cutting-edge criminological research about occupational choice and serial murder in *Chapter Five*.

We hope that you will use this textbook to inform your scholarly interest in the phenomenon of serial murder. We say this because we believe that what emerges from an academic understanding of the phenomenon of serial killing in Britain is that we need to learn that serial killers exploit fractured communities, in which some lives are seen as more valuable than others and where increasingly people have to struggle simply to survive. So too we must learn that serial killers make the most of police incompetence and public indifference to the young, vulnerable women who sell sexual services, or gay men who have a lifestyle that is seen to be challenging to the status quo; that they take advantage of the isolation, loneliness and powerlessness of the elderly; and that they exploit the public policies of successive governments which no longer sees value in the young or the old, and which prioritise the rich over the poor.

In other words, we study serial killing and serial killers because in their actions we begin to understand better our culture, our values and our civic society. For us, serial killing emerges as the elephant in the sitting room of public policies that create a culture of "them" and "us" and a society where there is a widening gap between the "haves" and the "have nots". In such societies it is presumed that some people simply don't have value for the development of that society, and can therefore be cast adrift as challenging the status quo and unrepresentative, or as a burden on the state's resources. It is these circstances and those groups that are characterised in this way that serial killers target.

This might all be a very long way from the fictional Clarice Starling interviewing Dr Hannibal Lector, the uses of offender profiling in police investigations, or the development of serial killer typologies—all of which might have initially prompted your interest in this subject—but we suggest that the materials that we will present to you and the arguments that we will make, are far more interesting and challenging than any of these fictional characters or investigatory techniques.

Using this Textbook

Throughout this textbook—including within this *Introduction*—we will introduce you to a number of ideas and issues which you might not have previously considered about serial killers and the phenomenon of serial murder. We will flag these ideas and issues within each chapter by drawing your attention to some "Key Terms" that you should attempt to become familiar with and with a revision section at the end of each chapter to re-enforce your reading. We will also suggest other reading that you might like to consider to develop any themes which have been at the heart of each specific chapter.

However, having taught students for many years, we have tried to keep academic references to their barest minimum. Our students tell us that these simply get in the way of their reading and, as the more observant of you will have already noted, that there are in fact only two references in this introduction! Even so, it is important to remember that the materials that are being presented to you have been developed from our own work and that of other scholars and, at the very least, you need to be aware of who wrote that work; how those authors sustained their argument(s); and what evidence they brought to bear on their materials. As such we have provided a guide to *Further Reading* at the end of each chapter which should be consulted for fuller references. Note too, because of this seeming student aversion to using academic references, we have usually provided the complete reference within the text.

Revision

- Why do you think the press was so interested in the crimes committed by Joanne Dennehy? Suggest at least three factors which made her case unusual.
- Provide one example of the disproportionate use made by fiction of the phenomenon of serial murder.
- What is meant by a "protective frame"?

Further Reading

Some of the ideas presented in this *Introduction* were taken from a colletion of essays about serial murder by S Waller (ed.) (2010) *Serial Killers: Philosophy for Everyone*, Oxford: Wiley-Blackwell. For those of you who would like to pursue these ideas further, have a look at the chapter by Eric Dietrich and Tara Fox Hall called "The Allure of the Serial Killer", pp.93–102.

There were two specific references within the chapter. F Brookman (2005) *Understanding Homicide*, London: Sage and D Wilson (2009) *A History of British Serial Killing*, London: Sphere.

WHAT IS SERIAL MURDER? 1

What's Montague? It is nor hand, nor foot,
Nor arm, nor face, nor any other part
Belonging to a man. O, be some other name!
What's in a name? That which we call a rose
By any other name would smell as sweet.

Romeo and Juliet, William Shakespeare, Act II, Scene 2

As we started to discuss within the *Introduction,* on what basis should we decide what is and what is not serial murder? To help answer this question, we have also introduced the idea of there being at least two elements which should contribute to making a decision — a numeric threshold in terms of the numbers of victims, and an element of time. Seeking to identify serial killers in this way would, for example, allow us to decide if Joanne Dennehy is, or is not a "serial killer" and, more generally, to differentiate between those people who might murder a very large number of people, but in one incident where there is no "cooling-off" period, and those murderers whom we call serial killers. But how many victims should there be, and how long is this element of time — the "cooling-off" period — that we have alluded to? Are there other issues that we should also consider, and might some people, agencies or indeed governments benefit from looser (or tighter) definitions of what we mean when we label someone as a "serial killer"?

This chapter takes as its focus historic and more recent debates about how to define serial murder, and considers how this definition has changed over time and between different cultures. It also uses the example of how the Federal Bureau of Investigation (FBI) in the USA used the phenomenon of serial murder for its own benefit in the 1980s. The chapter begins by putting the phenomenon of serial murder into the wider context of homicide and murder in England and Wales and begins by providing a basic definition of murder.

Murder and Homicide Defined

Let's start with a confession. Defining "murder" is fraught with as many difficulties as defining "serial murder". This difficulty has not been eased by the fact that there has been surprisingly little rigorous academic attention paid to murder, to the extent that Fiona Brookman (2005: 1) has gone as far as to claim that the broader subject of homicide has suffered from "academic neglect". As a consequence questions related to explaining what motivates one human being to kill another human being are rarely considered in criminology or psychology, despite the widespread fascination that this type of question generates more popularly. And what would an attempt to answer the question of motivation look like? Should we consider the wider social structure in which the murder has taken place, and into which the murderer has been socialised? In other words, is there a relationship between murder and, for example, poverty, gender, or race? Or, do these "macro" issues become less important in answering this question of motivation when we consider the "micro" level of the dynamics of the crime itself? Are murderers "pathological"—different, in some way from us, or are the roots of violence and murder far more widespread and common than we care to acknowledge? These are all important questions which we will consider in these first two chapters, but let's first try to define murder.

The classic definition of murder has been attributed to Sir Edward Coke and is embedded in the Offences Against the Person Act 1861. This stated that:

> "Murder is when a man of sound memory, and of the age of discretion, unlawfully killest within any county of the realm any creature in rerum natura under the King's peace, with malice aforethought, either expressed by the party or implied by law, so as the party wounded or hurt etc. die of the wound or hurt etc. within a year and a day after the same."

The only substantive change to this definition in England and Wales has been to remove the "year and a day" rule in 1996, and the idea of "malice aforethought"—or *mens rea* (the guilty mind)—remains central within the legal definition of murder (see *Key Term—Mens Rea*). Murder, which requires an intention to kill another human being or similar state of mind is thus different from "homicide" which is a general term for any death caused to another person and would include not just murder but, for example, manslaughter or causing death by dangerous or careless driving (or in Scotland what is known as "culpable homicide").

Key Term — Mens Rea

Definition: This Latin term literally means "a guilty mind" and within the common law is concerned with the intent behind the act that was committed. It is sometimes more popularly characterised as to whether or not the perpetrator had "malice aforethought".

In very broad terms, at least in England and Wales, homicide is used generically to describe the killing of a human being by another regardless of motive, or whether the act was lawful or unlawful. Examples of lawful deaths, for example, might include deaths caused as a result of acts of war; or when a boxer kills his opponent. Killings which are unlawful include murder, manslaughter or infanticide (terms which suggest that there are different levels of culpability) and it is these unlawful killings which are the focus of this book. So, it should be noted that we are not discussing, for example, causing death by dangerous driving, those killed as a result of terrorist activities or, as Brookman observes:

> "...the slow and painful deaths of thousands of individuals exposed to pernicious dusts, such as asbestos, despite ample evidence, known to employers, of the potentially fatal health risks, or the negligent and

> fraudulent safety testing of drugs by the pharmaceutical industry, or environmental crimes that cause death due to the dumping of toxic waste and illegal toxic emissions, Brookman." (2005: 3)

What Brookman is describing here is the need to remember that how we define a certain act creates the contexts in which that act becomes understood. That understanding thereafter determines how that act should be responded to by, on the one hand, the legal system and, on the other, society more generally. To make an obvious point, far more people are killed each year on the roads in this country than are murdered, but we choose not to see deaths caused by dangerous driving in the same way that we view murders. We also worry about serial murder, rather than toxic waste being dumped in our seas, deforestation or man-made global warming all of which are far more troubling and potentially lethal than murder or even serial murder.

The need to acknowledge how definitions or, as Juliet would have it, the naming of things, shape our understanding of events, how we should manage them, and how defining them—or naming them as something else—provides a recurring context for this chapter. By way of illustration, let's consider the case of John Barr. Barr was responsible for the deaths of twenty-one people—many of them elderly—in Wishaw, Scotland, but the chances are that you will not have heard of him.

In November 1996 a group of pensioners gathered for lunch in their local church hall and ate stewed steak in puff pastry, all of which had been supplied by their local, prize-winning butcher, John M Barr and Son. Within weeks, six of the lunch party were dead—with more deaths to follow, and even today many others in Wishaw who had been supplied with meat from this same source still suffer from kidney problems and fatigue as a result of what has been described as the world's worst recorded outbreak of fatal E coli food poisoning.

In a report conducted into the events surrounding this outbreak, Sheriff Principal Graham Cox criticised Barr suggesting that he had only paid "lip service to environmental health officers so that he could conceal the full extent of his business operations. In this way he was able to avoid very tight food regulations set out in 1994," (BBC News, August 19 1998). Sheriff Cox also criticised local environmental health officers (EHOs) who had not issued Barr with an emergency prohibition notice, which would have immediately stopped the sale of cooked meat from his shop. As a result Barr was able to continue to supply more cooked meat a few days later to an 18th birthday party, where there were over 100 guests. When some of these guests started to fall ill, EHOs once again interviewed Barr but they did not record their meeting, make notes for a transcript, or caution Barr that anything that he said could be used in court. As a result, a trial in November 1997 against Barr for culpable, wilful and reckless supply of contaminated meat to the birthday party collapsed and, to date, Barr has simply been fined £2,250.

Barr's story is of interest because it is illustrative of a number of issues which we have started to consider and which are important to highlight before further considering how to define serial murder. First, it reminds us that what we call 'crime'—including violent, predatory crime such as murder—is socially constructed and rarely do we think of the small, local butcher's shop, much larger, multi-national corporations deliberately ignoring Health and Safety legislation, or indeed the State itself, as a source of unlawful homicide through, for example, leaking or dumping toxic waste.

Key Term — Social Construction

Definition: This concept suggests that what we call crime—including murder and serial murder—is decided by society. In other words behaviours are not fixed, objective realities but are defined and explained before they become "real". There will be some individuals and groups who as a result of their status, resources, power, organization and access to the mass media will have the ability to make their construction appear legitimate.

The law—and criminology—rarely deals with the deaths caused in this way as worthy of scrutiny, or as troublesome, problematic and unlawful. As a result there was and has been no moral panic about John Barr and nor, frankly, was there very much press interest, even though the twenty-one deaths that resulted from his sale of contaminated cooked meats would have ranked him third highest on our list of British serial killers since 1888, with more deaths attributable to him than Jack the Ripper, John Haigh, Reg Christie, Peter Manuel, Peter Sutcliffe, Dennis Nilsen, the Wests and Ian Brady and Myra Hindley.

Of course in thinking about these issues we need to remember *mens rea*—the "guilty mind"—that we have described above. *Mens rea* is the mental element in an offence, rather than its physical aspects. As for murder, it covers a range of states of mind and so considers, for example, whether the person intended to kill another person, or whether that death was simply the result of negligence or recklessness. Here intention is the key issue to be considered and if a jury decides that a defendant deliberately set out to kill then that person would be found guilty of murder.

Deciding that someone is guilty of murder has serious consequences for the perpetrator, for anyone over the age of 21 who is convicted of murder is given a mandatory life sentence, and is usually described as being a "lifer". If someone is convicted of murder between the age of ten but under the age of 18 they are sentenced to detention during Her Majesty's pleasure, or custody for life if they were aged over 18 but under 21 at the time of the offence.

Having defined murder, raised a number of issues related to that definition and considered how society prioritises some deaths over others, let's now turn to serial murder.

Some Various and Early Definitions of Serial Murder

Serial killing is neither a modern nor a particularly North American phenomenon. However, when thinking about how to define serial murder it is perhaps best to consider how this type of murder came to the public's attention in the United States in the 1980s. In other words, how it came to be "socially constructed". We would suggest that an unique combination of politics, people, issues, events and industries served to "create" what we have now come to call serial murder. At the very least this combination of factors would include: media interest in serial killers, such as Ted Bundy and John Wayne Gacy; academic research about the phenomenon of serial murder; true crime and popular novels about this subject—such as Thomas Harris's *Red Dragon* (1981) and *The Silence of the Lambs* (1988); political use of voter concerns about violent crime; and the needs of one particular law enforcement agency—the FBI. Taken together, these diverse forces all served to ensure that serial murder became fixed in the popular imagination.

Amongst the academics who first wrote about serial murder were James DeBurger, Ronald Holmes, Stephen Holmes, Eric Hickey, Jack Levin, James Fox, Steve Egger, Philip Jenkins and Elliot Leyton (whom we will write more about in *Chapter Two*). As for defining what constituted serial murder, in their classic book about the subject, for example, Ronald Holmes and Stephen Holmes (1994) suggested, "A serial killer is defined as someone who murders three persons in more than a 30-day period. These killings typically involve one victim per episode," (p. 92). So too, a decade later, James Fox and Jack Levin (2005) in their book *Extreme Killing: Understanding Serial and Mass Murder* were still defining a serial killer as someone who killed three or more victims, and noted that he "may continue to kill over a period of months or years, often ha[ving] long time lapses between homicides, during which time he maintains a more or less ordinary life, going to work and spending time with family and friends" (p. 17).

These academics found support from a number of FBI agents—often located in the Behavioural Science Unit (BSU). The BSU had been founded in 1972 by an agent called Jack Kirsch and was then run by John Phaff, Roger DePue and, when DePue retired, by John Douglas. The BSU, which was later re-named as the Investigative Support Unit, was based at the FBI's Academy in Quantico, Virginia and it was to this academy that the fictional characters Will Graham in *Red Dragon* and Clarice Starling in *The Silence of the Lambs* were attached. The agents most popularly associated with the BSU included Robert Ressler, Ray Hazelwood and John Douglas, each of whom also described themselves as "profilers". These agents would gain considerable fame from writing true crime books, appearing on TV and radio and delivering public lectures, as well as writing, or contributing to more academic books.

More controversially, Ressler (who wrongly claimed to have coined the term "serial killer") was also engaged by the defence team representing the serial killer Jeffrey Dahmer and Douglas wrongly advised that an anonymous letter written by the "Green River Killer"—a serial killer who killed at least 48 women in Washington State in the early 1980s—should be ignored.

In their *Crime Classification Manual*, Douglas *et al* (1992) attempted to create an operational definition for several crimes, and within their classification of homicide was a subcategory of serial murder, which they defined as, "… three or more separate events in three or more separate locations with an emotional cooling-off period between homicides. The serial murder is hypothesised to be premeditated, involving offense-related fantasy and detailed planning." They go on:

> "When the time is right for him and he has cooled off from his last homicide, the serial killer selects his next victim, and proceeds with his plan. The cooling-off period can last for days, weeks, or months and is the key feature that distinguishes the serial killer from other multiple murderers." (Douglas *et al*: 96–97)

Taken together we can therefore see some consensus developing about how to define serial murder although, as you may have noticed, the latter definition about the "cooling-off period" has become somewhat less focussed ("days, weeks, or months"), even if the numeric threshold for the numbers of victims remains three or more.

Here it is also important to acknowledge that at this time the fictional work of Thomas Harris—who was given extraordinary access to the BSU—was widely acknowledged by both the academic community and by law enforcement as contributing towards the public's understanding of serial murder. For example, Ronald Holmes in the preface to *Serial Murder*, described how "I have also been fortunate enough to count Thomas Harris among my new friends." Holmes continues:

> "I have shared some meals with Tom, and I look at him and wonder where in his brain resides the characters he brings to the printed page. More than one time in the cases that I have profiled for police departments across the United States, I have uttered words similar to those of Will Graham: 'You had to touch her, didn't you?'" (Holmes and Holmes, 1994: x-xi).

So too Douglas was Harris's model for the fictional FBI Agent Jack Crawford in *Red Dragon* and *Silence of the Lambs* and, in his co-written book about the serial killer Dennis Rader—Douglas and Dodd (2007: 8) *Inside the Mind of BTK: The True Story Behind the Thirty-Year Hunt for the Notorious Wichita Serial Killer*—Douglas suggests, in a phrase that would not have been out of place in a novel, that "climbing inside the heads of monsters is my speciality." Frankly, it is not too hard to see where Harris had found some of the inspiration for his characters and how those characters in turn began to shape the reality of the people that they were supposedly based upon.

Dissenting Voices

Not all academics agreed with the definition of serial murder that was beginning to come to be accepted and there were a number of dissenting voices. Steve Egger (1990), for example, in *Serial Murder: An Elusive Phenomenon* argued that there is a six point identification of the serial killer and that a serial murder only occurs when:

> "(1) one or more individuals (in many cases, male) commit(s) a second murder and/or subsequent murder; (2) there is generally no prior rela-

> tionship between victim and attacker (if there is a relationship, such a relationship will place the victim in a subjugated role to the killer); (3) subsequent murders are at different times and have no apparent connection to the initial murder; and (4) are usually committed in a different geographical location. Further, (5) the motive is not for material gain and is for the murderer's desire to have power or dominance over his victims. (6) Victims may have symbolic value for the murderer and/or are perceived to be prestigeless and in most instances are unable to defend themselves or alert others to their plight, or are perceived as powerless given their situation in time, place, or status within their immediate surroundings, examples being vagrants, the homeless, prostitutes, migrant workers, homosexuals, missing children, single women (out by themselves), elderly women, college students, and hospital patients." (p. 5-6)

In essence Egger was suggesting that there should only be two victims; that the murders should occur at different locations; and crucially that there should be no relationship between the victim and the perpetrator. Is this definition too precise, or too loose? Perhaps it's both. In a British context it would, for example, exclude some perpetrators such as Dennis Nilsen and Fred and Rosemary West, who all clearly had a prior relationship with many of their victims, and who murdered them in the same locations in London and Gloucester respectively. In this sense Egger's definition is too prescriptive. However, by reducing the numbers of victims to two instead of three, such British murderers as Graham Young—who murdered his two victims by poisoning them and who attempted to poison several more—would become a "serial killer". In this way Egger's definition is too loose, as it would create more "serial killers".

So too, based on Egger's definition, we could call Benjamin Geen and Paul Brumfitt serial killers, although each of these British cases poses yet more definitional issues. Geen, for example, was a nurse who murdered two of his patients in January 2004, by deliberately administering fatal overdoses of drugs. At his trial at Oxford Crown Court in 2006 it was alleged that he tried to kill at least 16 other patients. While he did not have a prior relationship with his victims, each of these murders was committed in the same location—as Hickey would describe it, they were "place specific"—and therefore would not pass Egger's threshold. Geen's case also reminds us that some of our most prolific serial killers have been healthcare professionals and we discuss occupational choice and serial murder in *Chapter Five*. Brumfitt, on the other hand, killed two men in the 1970s in the same incident—allegedly because they made gay advances towards him (personal communication)—served a sentence of 15 years, and then on release killed again, only this time a female sex worker. Does the time gap between his first and last victim push the definition of a "cooling-off period" too far for his inclusion? Can this last murder be seen as part of a "series" given the difference in the gender of his victims?

The Use of Serial Murder

The most vociferous of the original dissenting voices about serial killing as a phenomenon belongs to Philip Jenkins. Jenkins (1994) argued in *Using Murder: The Social Construction of Serial Homicide* that serial murder accounted for perhaps less than one per cent of all American homicides, which would equate to some 200 deaths per year. Nonetheless this phenomenon had been "exploited by a wide variety of official agencies and interest groups, and the issue has been used as a multifaceted weapon in political debate" (p. 3). He suggested that serial murder had been presented by these various interest groups as novel and unprecedented and that the threat posed by serial murderers was suggested to be all the greater because serial killers were viewed as highly mobile, wandering freely between different states and legal jurisdictions. This latter suggestion therefore gave greater authority to the federal (as opposed to state) Justice Department to claim that it needed to expand its bureaucratic and law enforcement operations, with associated increases in personnel, financial resources and public and political prestige.

The basis for making the claims that the Justice Department promoted was a research programme within the FBI's Behavioural

Science Unit—led by Ressler—called the Criminal Personality Research Project. In effect what the FBI had wanted to do was to find a way to use the wealth of forensic information that they were able to generate from crime scenes and see if from that evidence they could suggest something of the type of offender who had committed the offence. So, in part using their collective experience of investigating multiple murder and sexual assaults and, crucially through carrying out extensive interviews with 36 convicted murderers, 25 of whom were serial killers, they began to assert that the personality of an offender—in cases of serial rape or murder—could be gleaned from a consideration of the following five areas: the crime scene; the nature of the attacks themselves; forensic evidence; a medical examination of the victim; and victim characteristics. These interviews (and see the following chapter) and the analyses that flowed from them, were the beginning of what we have come to know as "profiling".

On the back of this research programme, the FBI made a number of statements which captured the public's attention and also served to garner political support. For example, the Justice Department alleged that as many as 4,000 Americans per year—about 20 per cent of all homicide victims—were murdered by serial killers. Ressler himself suggested that "serial killing—I think that it's at epidemic proportions. The type of crime we're seeing today did not really occur with any known frequency prior to the fifties. [It] is a relatively new phenomenon in the crime picture of the U.S." (quoted in Jenkins, 1994: 67). So, given this "epidemic" and "new phenomenon" the Justice Department lobbied for—and then created—the National Centre for the Analysis of Violent Crime (NCAVC) and the Violent Criminal Apprehension Programme (VICAP), both of which are still in existence.

In 1996 the independent National Criminal Justice Commission (NCJC), in a report that they called *The Real War on Crime,* was able to offer some critical assessment about these various claims and statements about violent crime generally and serial murder in particular. The report claimed that "a hoax is afoot"; that the FBI had "hyped" the threats posed by serial killers; and that the true extent of murder that could be attributed to serial killers per year was between 50 to 60 — still quite a large figure, but nowhere near the terrifying levels of 4,000. Indeed, what the NCJC was able to show was that the figure of 4,000 related to unsolved murders and that all of these had simply been attributed by the FBI to murders committed by serial killers (Donziger (ed.), 1996: 2; 76–79).

Here too we should remember that this period also saw the rapid growth of the prison population in the USA. The numbers of people being imprisoned, for example, increased from just under 500,000 in 1980 to just over 1,500,000 by 1994. Some of that growth can be attributed to specific initiatives undertaken within particular states and more nationally, and which were given shape and support by the adoption of a "right realist" law and order agenda, which had become more strident with the election of Ronald Reagan as President in 1980. These so-called "get tough" initiatives included, for example, "zero-tolerance" policing; "truth in sentencing"; and, more famously, "three strikes and you're out". Each served to ensure that the prison population increased.

However, as *The Real War on Crime* explains, this series of policies could be characterised as "bait and switch". In other words, they appeared to be focussed on locking up violent offenders in a fight against crime, but in fact simply filled American prisons with non-violent and petty offenders, who posed no risk to the public and could easily have been managed within the community (Donziger (ed.), 1996: 18). Within this type of febrile political climate, talk about "serial killers" helped serve to keep law and order at the top of the policy agenda and, as one recent critic has put it, also "elevated the members of the FBI's then Behavioural Science Unit to super-star status" (Turvey, 2012: 608).

More Recent Definitions — Cooling-off?

This early consensus — notwithstanding the dissenting voices that we have acknowledged — was based around defining serial murder as involving three victims and that there should be a "cooling-off period" between each killing. As we have seen, this latter component was variously (sometimes loosely) defined but, in essence referred to the period when the killer disconnected from the behaviours that had led them to commit murder and to re-integration into their non-offending lives and activities. It is this "cooling-off period" — the element of time — that therefore differentiates serial murder from spree or mass murder, given that in these types of murders the killer does not disconnect from killing.

This early consensus did not last. Specifically, in July 2008, for example, the FBI, as a result of a symposium that they had held in 2005, revised their definition of serial murder to be the "unlawful killing of two or more victims by the same offender(s), in separate events". So, the numbers of victims required for an offender to be labelled as a serial killer was reduced from three to two and the "cooling-off period" was re-formulated as simply involving murders that were committed as "separate events". This we suggest is a very imprecise way to define "serial murder". By this definition, for example, a murder committed by an offender in the morning and another later that same day could be viewed as "separate events" and so the perpetrator labelled as a "serial killer." We suggest that this broadens our understanding of the phenomenon of serial murder so far as to render it indistinguishable from other types of murder.

This most recent definition by the FBI also suggests that the "cooling-off period" has become less important in the definition of serial murder. Indeed Brent Turvey (2012), writing in *Criminal Profiling* has argued that the cooling-off period can be "immediate — as instant as flipping a switch" (p. 543). However, if we were to accept this type of reasoning, it really would be impossible to differentiate serial from spree or mass murder, although gamely Turvey argues that spree or mass murderers, unlike serial killers, "resign themselves" to killing and "do not come back until … they have been stopped" (p. 543). No evidence is presented to support this assertion.

Other Definitional Issues to Consider

So far we have concentrated on defining serial murder by considering a numeric threshold in relation to the numbers of victims and an element of time—which is usually referred to as a "cooling-off period". But how should we think about forms of repeated murder that might result from terrorism or "contract killing"? In short, are "hitmen" and terrorists also serial killers? Let's consider these issues to further test how we should define what it is that we mean when we label someone as a serial killer.

A hitman can be defined as a person who accepts an order (a contract) to kill another human being from someone who is not publicly acknowledged as a legitimate authority regarding legally sanctioned killing as when, for example, soldiers kill, or the death penalty is exacted by state executioners. In other words, the context in which contract killing occurs involves a "distance" between the victim and the perpetrator—a distance, moreover, that is not present in conventional murder. Crucially we also need to acknowledge that the motive—in other words what is driving the hitman to behave in a certain way—is "extrinsic", rather than "intrinsic".

Extrinsic motivation comes from outside of the individual and is an external pressure on the individual to perform an act to obtain a desired outcome. The external pressure in this context is, most obviously, the financial reward given to the hitman for carrying out the hit, but we might also see political or religious beliefs, as when a terrorist commits murder in the hope of obtaining a greater political goal as being extrinsic. On the other hand intrinsic motivation refers to motivations that are driven by an interest or enjoyment in the task itself and does not rely on any external pressures to complete the task. In short, serial killers are intrinsically motivated, while hitmen, terrorists, soldiers and state executioners are extrinsically motivated.

Serial Killers Defined!

As we indicated in our *Introduction* accurately defining the phenomenon that we are seeking to describe is very important for a number of reasons. For example, accurately defining what we mean when we label someone as a serial killer allows us to gain an insight into how widespread serial murder might be, and therefore in a better position to judge how to appropriately allocate resources aimed at combating this type of murder. So too an accurate definition will allow law enforcement agencies to identify trends which helps with case linkage in specific cases and more general trends—such as particular victim groups that are vulnerable to attack. An accurate definition of serial murder can help assuage public fears that this type of murder has reached "epidemic" proportions which, in turn, allows the public to better judge the claims that some politicians might make about "law and order" and the need to "get tough". Finally, an accurate definition—a proper baseline if you prefer—allows us to make more scholarly and academic analyses by testing hypotheses and building theory.

On the other hand, loosely defining any phenomenon, or allowing that definition to be shaped or bent or moulded to suit the needs of individuals, groups, or industries leaves the way clear for these various groups to make claims that are difficult to challenge, or indeed disprove. The door is left open for the phenomenon—in the words of NCJC—to become "hyped".

Given all of this we have chosen to continue to define serial murder as three or more murders which are committed in a period of greater than 30 days, with a cooling-off period between each event. There will be some who will criticise this definition as being too loose and others who will say that we are being too prescriptive. Too loose because we do not accept Egger's argument that these murders should be in separate locations but, on the other hand, too prescriptive because we have kept the numeric threshold at three victims, rather than two. We have also used the "cooling-off" period of 30 days, which again will be seen by some as prescriptive. However, we believe that serial murder is qualitatively different to multiple or spree murders and what it is that differentiates these phenomena is the ability of the serial killer to inhabit two different worlds. He kills and then re-integrates back into society. Indeed, it is this ability that makes serial murderers of criminological interest and which also produces such disbelieving reactions by members of the public when it is revealed that the man that they played golf with, or lived next door to or had as their GP, was in fact a serial killer.

We do not argue that our definition is perfect, or that it can simply be applied without any exercise of judgment. For example, we provided earlier the example of Paul Brumfitt, who did in fact commit three murders in a period of greater than 30 days. However, his "cooling-off period" between the three murders which he committed was separated by a long period of imprisonment. Can he really be viewed as a "serial" killer? So too, he killed two of his three victims in one incident. Does this not also change how his actions should be viewed? For us it does, although there will be others who will disagree. However, at the very least, we have been open about how we have arrived at this definition and also consistent, for this has been how we have described serial murder in our scholarly work about this subject and which has allowed us to develop theories based on this phenomenon.

That leaves us with Joanne Dennehy. Is she a "serial killer"? There will be some who will argue that she is and, if we were to apply the FBI's most recent definition, they would be accurate. However, as we have shown, it would be equally correct to describe her as a spree killer or as a mass murderer. If we used our definition then Dennehy is not a serial killer. While her behaviour was appalling and she has rightly been imprisoned under a whole life sentence, there was no 30 day "cooling-off period" during her killings and it is this which we suggest means that she is a spree killer. This conclusion might not satisfy everyone, especially those who are in the business of turning serial murder into a commodity—something that can be used to generate resources, or wealth. After all, the label "serial killer" is scary, sexy and, sadly, it sells. By using this definition, we have chosen not to play on any popular fears, or exaggerate the extent of the phenomenon.

Revision

- Why is *mens rea* so important to our understanding of murder?
- How does the story of John Barr help us to understand how murder and serial murders are social constructions?

- Explain how the FBI benefitted from the public's understanding of serial murder.
- How should we define what is or is not a "serial murder".

Further Reading

A number of books were cited throughout this chapter and reading these for yourselves will allow you to follow the arguments that we have made more closely. We have also described—but not cited—our own work. A quick introduction to this would be D Wilson (2009) *A History of British Serial Killing*, London: Sphere (including in relation to matters not cited in full here). You might also like to read Thomas Harris's novels which were so central in creating the public's impression of what serial murder was and what could be done to combat this type of crime.

THEORETICAL PERSPECTIVES ON SERIAL MURDER

2

> "You may want to believe that a biological basis to violence does not exist, or it is going to be explained away in some manner. Like an ostrich evading the hunter, you may decide to bury your head in the sand. But if you do not make a move and act on the anatomy of violence, I believe this cancer will continue. And you had better watch out—the ostrich may get shot."
>
> Adrian Raine (2013), *The Anatomy of Violence: The Biological Roots of Crime*, p. 373.

> "The summer of 1981 was the first summer for over 40 years that a young man living in a poor area would find work or training very scarce, and it got worse in the years that followed. When the recession of the 1980s hit, mass unemployment was concentrated on the young, they were simply not recruited. Over time the harm caused in the summer of 1981 was spread a little more evenly, life became more difficult for slightly older men, most of the younger men were, eventually, employed. However, the seeds that were sown then, that date at which something changed to lead to the rise in murders in the rest of the 1980s and 1990s, can still be seen through the pattern of murder by age and year." Danny Dorling, (2006) "Prime Suspect: Murder in Britain," *Prison Service Journal*, July No. 166, p 9.

This chapter is concerned with the two dominant academic, theoretical traditions that are employed to inform an understanding about serial murder. We describe these two paradigms as the "medico-psychological" and the "structural" traditions and we offer two views at the very start of this chapter from Professors Adrian Raine and Danny Dorling which perfectly capture their differences. However, to be fair, we should note that in the quote that we use Raine is advocating for, almost pleading with his readers, to accept the broader principle of there being a more general biological basis for violence, rather than serial murder, although he has also a great deal to say about murderers and serial killers. On the other hand Dorling, rather more carefully, is attributing the rise in the number of murders — not serial murder — in Britain to social and economic changes that occurred in 1981 — a period dominated by "Thatcherism".

We should also remember that there are other ways to think about serial murder and various theories regarding individual serial killers are to be found within, for example, the "true crime" genre, and the hundreds of websites that are to be found on the net about serial murder and serial killers. However, we would suggest that most academic and serious commentators base their understanding of this phenomenon by searching for answers either through considering what it is that makes the serial killer different from the rest of us — in other words that which makes him "pathological"—or by considering the importance of the social structure(s) which produce more (or less) serial killers. The former is what we call the medico-psychological tradition, and the latter the structural tradition. Of course, in many ways, these traditions are based on familiar ideas. After all, debates about "nature or nurture"; are offenders "born or made"; or is an offender personally responsible for his crimes, as opposed to the responsibilities of society more generally, are central to the discipline of criminology.

We also discuss each of these two traditions to show how accepting one, or the other, leads to further consequences. For example, an acceptance that there is something pathological about individual serial killers and that that pathology can be identified at a crime scene is at the heart of what is known as "offender profiling". We discuss this more fully below and describe other forms of profiling.

On the other hand, a structural approach might emphasise a victim perspective, so as to demonstrate that only a few groups of people are regularly targeted by serial killers, because of some vulnerability in the victim group which can be exploited by this type of killer. So too, a structural approach might attempt to show that some countries, at particular times, produce more serial killers than other countries, or at different times within the same country, and seek to understand why this should be the case. This type of argument and analysis does not have a direct policing application—as with offender profiling—but is instead concerned with broader, political, economic, cultural and social change.

We have described these two traditions as dominant, but that does not necessarily mean that they are equal. Theorising based on the medico-psychological tradition, encompassing biology, brain functioning, genetic inheritance, personality and so forth—and which has its roots in positivism—is the most popular way to think about serial murder and garners most academic and wider interest and resources. Given that this is the case, we start by considering the medico-psychological tradition, before considering the structural tradition. However, our intention is not to take you through every twist and turn of these two traditions, which would be a book in itself! Rather, for the medico-psychological tradition we concentrate on how genetics and personality—especially "psychopathy"—are thought to play a role in creating the serial killer, and within the structural tradition we adopt a victim perspective and consider whether or not serial murder in Britain can be viewed as a form of "homicidal protest". This we have chosen these particular topics as illustrative of the two traditions.

Key Term — Positivism

Definition: Both a methodological approach to producing knowledge — based on the idea that it was possible to study society and social phenomena such as crime using methods derived from the natural sciences, and also a view that crime is committed by people who are somehow different from those who do not offend. This idea is most often associated with the Italian criminologist Cesare Lombroso (1836–1909) who suggested that offenders were "atavistic" — a throwback to an earlier form of human evolution and therefore had a number of physical characteristics which could be identified.

As the start of running threads to guide you through our description of the medico-psychological tradition we begin by introducing two articles, both published in the 1960s. The first, which appeared in *Nature* in 1965, with Patricia Jacobs as the lead author, was called "Aggressive Behaviour, Mental Sub-Normality and the XYY Male". This introduced the idea that there was something genetically different about violent men — an idea that has continued to interest a number of scientists. The second was called "The Threat to Kill" and was published in the *American Journal of Psychiatry* by the forensic psychiatrist John Marshall Macdonald, who argued that a "triad" of three traits — fire-setting, cruelty to animals and bed-wetting — were the keys to understanding who would become violent. This is sometimes known as "the Macdonald triad" or the "homicidal triad" and is the beginning of an interest in how personality might create or shape the direction of the violent offender.

Medical-Psychological — Genetic Inheritance and Personality

By 2000 an international group of scientists had finished a working draft of the human genome. Three years later they provided a complete one, and further analysis is still being undertaken. This has led to all sorts of rather fanciful speculation that some day it will be possible to identify a "criminal gene". However, even as early as the 1960s a number of genetic abnormalities had already been found in human cells and among these was a condition called XYY—which is perhaps the first popularly thought of "criminal gene".

Humans normally have twenty-three pairs of chromosomes and each chromosome is made up of a number of genes. One of these chromosomes determines gender. Women normally have two X chromosomes (and they are therefore XX) and men have one X and one Y (and are therefore XY). Researchers discovered that a small proportion of the male population had an extra Y chromosome, which meant that they had double the male chromosomes normally found in men and so they were popularly labelled as having "supermale syndrome". In 1965 research published in *Nature* demonstrated that a number of Scottish prisoners at the Secure State Hospital in Carstairs had an extra Y chromosome, which led to more general claims that XYY males were over-represented in prisons and appeared to have a propensity for violent crime.

This all became a matter of popular debate when a serial killer called Richard Speck killed eight student nurses, from the South Chicago Community Hospital in their dormitory, in July 1966. Speck took each of the nurses out of the dormitory one-by-one and led them into another room so that he could rape and strangle them. This behaviour provided an opportunity for one of the nurses in the dormitory, Corazon Amurao, to slide under a bed and hide. Speck, who was high on a combination of drugs and alcohol, did not realise that one of the nurses was missing and left the dormitory after he had killed eight victims. Corazon was later able to identify Speck as the killer.

XYY now enters the story. It was claimed by his defence team that Speck was XYY and there was some superficial justification for this claim. Speck, for example, was taller than average, had a learning disability and acne—all of which were seen as symptoms of XYY. This claim received wide publicity and even though it was proven that Speck was not XYY, it became almost folklore that violence could be linked to XYY males. There is no evidence to support this claim, although there is some evidence to suggest that men with XYY do commit more crime than men with XY. This has not stopped an interest in discovering a genetic cause for violent crime and Raine argues that "there are many genes other than those on the Y chromosome that likely play a role in criminal behaviour" (Raine, 2013: 50).

Raine, an Englishman who is a Professor at the University of Pennsylvania, has been almost messianic in his determination to prove that the roots of crime—especially violent crime—are genetic. As such he has also had a great deal to say about murder and serial murder and even goes as far as to suggest that he emigrated to the United States because "there were plenty of murderers who could be recruited into my research studies." Raine describes this research in a chapter of his book which he calls "Murderous Minds" and asks "would the brain scan of a murderer look like yours? Where exactly in the brain would the difference be? How would the brain functioning of serial killers ... differ from ... [the] more common variety of one-off killers" (Raine, 2013: 65–66). In short, not so much an XYY chromosome abnormality, but rather a difference, based on his research, which suggests that there is something different with the brains of killers.

Raine's particular research tool has been positron-emission-tomography, which is usually known as a "PET scan". In his study of 41 murderers, he discovered that there was a lack of activation in their prefrontal cortex and argued that it is this that explains their violent offending. He suggests that impairment in the prefrontal cortex would result in, for example, an inability to control anger and rage; a greater willingness to engage in rule-breaking behaviour; poor social judgement; a lack of problem-solving skills; and, finally, a host of personality issues such as impulsivity and a loss of self-control. All of these factors, he suggests, explains why this sample committed murder.

These 41 murderers were "one-off killers", as Raine describes them, rather than serial killers. However, he did have access to a PET scan of one serial killer—Randy Kraft. Kraft, also known as the "Freeway Killer," was found guilty of murdering at least 16 young men, some of whom were gay (as was Kraft), and others who could be described as "drifters", mostly in California, between 1972 and 1983. He is suspected of having killed many more. At his trial in 1989 a PET scan was introduced by his defence team and it is this scan that Raine has been able to analyse. He reveals that there is in fact no evidence of reduced prefrontal cortex functioning, as there was with the one-off killers, but somewhat more activation in that part of Kraft's brain called the thalamus. However, not to be deflected, Raine uses this result to explain how it was that Kraft had been able to avoid detection for as long as he did (as opposed to the one-off killers) because, he suggests, his excellent prefrontal cortex functioning allowed him to carefully plan and then adapt his killing strategy.

This does raise a very important issue. How do some serial killers evade detection, while others are caught relatively quickly? Raine wants to explain this by good or poor brain functioning. However he does not describe the circumstances in which his one-off killers came to murder and who might therefore never have intended to kill again. Nor does he have the evidence of PET scans from other serial killers to see if their scans showed good or bad prefrontal cortex functioning. In other words he has not been able to compare Kraft's PET scan with the scans of other serial killers. We might also note the types of victims that Kraft targeted and consider whether their disappearance and deaths would have generated the same police activity that, for example, the disappearance and murder of a young child might have produced. Might it have been his choice of victim which allowed him to continue killing for as long as he did? This is an issue which we will consider more fully when describing the structural tradition.

In describing the poor functioning of the prefrontal cortex of his one-off killers, Raine is implying that it was this that had had a major impact in determining their personality—that range of personal attributes and behaviours that are seen to characterise an individual. Do personality and the associated concept of an individual having a "personality disorder" explain why some people are capable of murder? "Personality disorder", after all, implies that the behaviours and personal attributes of the person labelled in this way give him or her, and more likely other people, cause for concern. In other words, those with personality disorders are seen to have behaviour that is unacceptable and antisocial. If we accept his analysis, Raine's one-off killers had personalities that were characterised by impulsivity and poor self-control, so that they could not inhibit their behaviour—rage, anger, or impulse to kill—appropriately. So might personality be the key to understanding murder and serial murder?

Perhaps the start of this line of reasoning within the medico-psychological tradition dates back to the so-called Macdonald "triad" of behaviours that were seen to be predictive of violence, because of the perpetrator's psychological maladjustment. This triad was made up of: animal cruelty; fire starting; and bed-wetting. Macdonald's paper relied on his clinical observation of 48 aggressive and sadistic patients who had threatened to kill someone, compared with 52 non-psychotic patients who had also threatened to kill someone. The ages of his sample ranged from eleven to 83. Given that his sample size was small and unrepresentative Macdonald himself did not believe that his study had any predictive value. Note too that his sample involved people who had made threats to kill, rather than people who had actually murdered. Even so, this has not stopped a number of people from assuming that the Macdonald triad's predictive power has been proven—in part because the FBI were often champions of Macdonald's conclusions. We discuss the FBI's own research with serial killers below. As for this triad of behaviours, they are probably more revealing of a stressed child in need of better support and guidance, rather than revealing the origins of a future serial killer.

The most recent and influential contributions about serial killers and personality are mostly related to the personality disorder called psychopathy. Psychopathy is characterised by a constellation of interpersonal, affective and behavioural characteristics, many of which were perhaps first described by Hervey Cleckley in 1941. What was of especial interest to Cleckley was the seeming disconnect between the air of sociability and competence that could be displayed by psychopaths, and the reality of their essential emptiness. In other words, psychopaths could be outwardly charming and relaxed, while in actual fact they were fundamentally untrustworthy and unreliable. However, to bring some precision to what was meant when someone was diagnosed as being a "psychopath" Robert Hare (1991) refined Cleckley's criteria to develop a Psychopathy Checklist, which he later revised and which is therefore known as the "PCL-R". The PCL-R has three core factors. The first relates to interpersonal deficits, such as glibness and manipulativeness; the second to emotional deficits, which would include, for example, callousness and lack of remorse; while the third set of factors consider behavioural deficits such as irresponsibility, need for stimulation and impulsivity.

Key Term — PCL-R

Definition: The PCL-R is a standardised instrument which yields a quantitative score concerning the degree of psychopathy of an individual by utilising a clinical interview and a comprehensive review of records. The instrument is scored on a 20-item, 40-point scale, where the individual is scored 0 if the item does not fit; 1 if there is a partial fit; and 2 if there is a reasonable fit. The validated research cut-off for determination of a psychopathic personality is a score of 25 in Britain and 30 or above in the USA.

However, before going further down this particular line of argument, we need to remember that it is perfectly possible for people who score highly on the PCL-R still to be able to function successfully in the community without ever resorting to crime. Indeed, a popular and developing field of the literature in recent years has focused upon the "corporate psychopath". These individuals, whilst still displaying similar interpersonal, affective and behavioural characteristics of their criminal counterparts, exist in a wholly different and non-violent social environment, arguably serving the needs of advanced capitalist economies, where a preoccupation with profit and economic growth is prioritised over welfare and wellbeing. Nonetheless, in our own work, we have found that psychopathy is a helpful way to understand a number of issues that have to be considered when thinking about serial killers. For example, how do they gain access to their victims? It makes more sense to imagine that someone who has a plausible, charming and manipulative personality is more likely to entice another person to accept a lift in their car, or to go home with them after an evening out, than an offender who is quite clearly deranged or violent. It also helps to explain why those people who knew serial killers find it so difficult to accept that their neighbour, the person that they played golf with, or their local GP was in fact someone who repeatedly killed. We consider this personality disorder more fully when describing the case of Mary Ann Cotton. However, once again, within the medico-psychological tradition, it is important to assess the contribution of the FBI and their approach to what became known as "offender profiling".

The FBI and their "Blunt Little Tool"

While there remain some lively debates about what actually constitutes "offender profiling" and how it should be defined, underlying most definitions is a belief that an offender's characteristics can be deduced from how he commits the offence. In other words, we can tell something about the personality of the offender from looking carefully at the offence characteristics gleaned from the following five areas: the crime scene; the nature of the attacks themselves; forensic evidence; a medical examination of the victim; and victim characteristics. Indeed at one stage offender profiling was sometimes also called "criminal personality profiling". This approach was developed by the FBI and their Criminal Personality Research Project, which was a study of 36 incarcerated offenders—of whom 25 were serial killers and eleven were sexual murderers who had committed one or two murders.

Little is known about the 36 interviews that the FBI conducted. However John Douglas, in his rather odd (for example, he compares himself to the fictional six-year-old boy Cole Sear who saw dead people in the 1999 film *The Sixth Sense*) and co-written 2007 book called *Inside the Mind of BTK: The True Story Behind the Thirty-Year*

Hunt for the Notorious Wichita Serial Killer, describes the fact that their interview protocol involved "thousands of questions" and ran to 57 pages in length (Douglas and Dodd, 2007: 4). It was this that the fictional serial killer Hannibal Lector dismissed as a "blunt little tool" in an exchange with Clarice Starling in *The Silence of the Lambs*. Many of the FBI's questions were aimed at providing some basic information about the killer's motivation, victim selection, and the impact that the murders might have had on the killer. It would also appear that the FBI agents set out to answer whether or not their interviewees were "born to kill", or whether, for example, some childhood trauma had influenced their behaviour. The fruits of these interviews eventually led to the publication of Ressler, Burgess and Douglas's *Sexual Homicide: Patterns and Motives* in 1988.

Douglas provides a glimpse of how one of these interviews was conducted in 1981 when he visited Attica Correctional Facility in New York with Robert Ressler to interview David Berkowitz—also known as the "Son of Sam". Berkowitz is an American serial killer and arsonist who murdered six people and wounded seven others in New York between July 1976 until his arrest in August 1977. Douglas explains that he and Ressler had gone to Attica to "pry information out of the head of one of the nation's most notorious serial killers." He continues:

> "We'd arrived unannounced, on a fishing expedition of sorts, hoping to convince David Berkowtiz, aka Son of Sam, to help us with our criminal profiling study, which involved a fifty-seven-page interview questionnaire. We wanted answers to such questions as *What was his motive? Was there a trigger that set him off on his murderous spree? What was his early childhood like? How did he select his victims? Did he ever visit the grave sites of his victims? How closely did he follow the press coverage of his crimes?* His answers would help us better understand the killers we were hunting." (Douglas and Dodd, 2007: 19, emphasis in original).

Seemingly, Berkowtiz was brought to see Douglas and Ressler who were waiting for him in a tiny interrogation room, although as the following exchange reveals it is clear that Berkowtiz had no idea who Douglas or Ressler were, or what they wanted.

'Who are you guys?' he asked the moment he spotted us seated at the far end of the only piece of furniture in the room—a linoleum-covered table. As planned, the guards had quickly exited before Berkowitz had a chance to tell us to take a hike. 'We're FBI agents, David' I told him. 'We'd like to talk to you. We're hoping you might be able to help us ... It's like I always say,' I explained, 'if you want to learn how to paint, you don't read about it in a book. You go straight to the artist. And that's what you are, David. You're the artist ... you're famous. You're huge. You had all of New York scared shitless. In a hundred years, no one will remember my name. But everybody will still know who the Son of Sam was (Douglas and Dodd, 2007: 19–20).

This flattery seems to have worked, for Douglas suggests that Berkowitz became "putty in our hands" and over the course of the next five hours "he walked us through every dark, twisted corner of his sad life, sharing details he'd never told anyone" (Douglas and Dodd, 2007: 20).

Douglas does not tell the reader what these details might have been and so there is no way of validating this claim, and nor is it revealed if Berkowtiz actually completed the fifty-seven-page questionnaire that formed the basis of Douglas and Ressler's research. Indeed, they seem to have simply chatted for a number of hours. However, there are more worrying issues that this account reveals, if this is indeed an accurate depiction of the interview(s). Ignoring the (absence of) ethics of the origin and conduct of the interview, for example, let's simply consider how credulous Douglas and Ressler seem to have been when they interviewed Berkowitz. After all, Berkowtiz, at the time of this interview three years into a 365 year sentence, might have had a variety of reasons for agreeing to be interviewed, after he realised that was in fact why he had been taken to the interrogation room, rather than simply falling for Douglas's flattery.

Should we not also consider whether serial killers necessarily tell an interviewer the truth? Might they attempt to confuse, or alternatively be over-eager in the hope of getting some sort of favour such as parole, a better work detail, or simply a more favourable cell allocation? That Douglas, Ressler an\d the other FBI agents interviewed serial killers who were caught may suggest something about this small sample and their offending behaviour, but all of this might have been very different from those offenders who remained at large and who might have used other approaches—approaches which allowed them to remain at large.

Even so, the FBI's central finding was that it was possible to determine through what became known as "crime scene analysis" whether that crime scene was "organized" or "disorganized" and that this dichotomy could be used to suggest something about the offender's personality in his everyday life. For example, an "organized" offender would be above average intelligence, sexually and socially competent and living with a partner. On the other hand, a disorganized offender would typically be someone who lives alone, who is sexually and socially inadequate and who would live quite close to the crime scene.

Key Term — Crime Scene Analysis: Organized/Disorganized

Definition: According to the FBI an *organized* crime scene is more clearly planned and both the victim and the crime scene itself are controlled. Very little forensic evidence will be found and the body of the victim will often be hidden. On the other hand a *disorganized* crime scene displays very little evidence of planning and as a result a great deal of forensic evidence can be gathered. Usually the victim's body is left in such a way that it can be easily found. Often there are sexual acts performed on the victim after death.

There have been a number of criticisms of the FBI's approach—some of which we have already alluded to. Of the remainder, we should note the current and lively debates that continue to be discussed about what is known as the "homology assumption" and the "behavioural consistency hypothesis". The former implies that different offenders who perform the same types of crimes will have similar personal traits or characteristics; the latter hypothesis suggests that the offender's personality will not change over time and therefore he will continue to commit crimes in a roughly similar way. Research on these assumptions has generally shown that the homological assumption cannot really be sustained, although there is evidence to suggest that, by and large, an offender will continue to offend in a similar way and so the crime scene will contain behavioural clues that may be identified as the "signature" of that offender.

Apart from crime scene analysis there have been at least two other approaches to offender profiling which have gained prominence. These two approaches are called "investigative psychology" and "geographic profiling". Investigative psychology is most closely associated with Professor David Canter, who has done much to make what has become known as "profiling" much more scientifically rigorous. In contrast to the FBI's "top down" approach to crime scene analysis—in effect relying on the skill and experience of the analyst—Canter has advocated for a "bottom up" approach to offender profiling, using psychological theory and statistical analysis to assess evidence from the crime scene with which to develop a profile of the likely offender. Geographic profiling is also associated with investigative psychology. It developed in the 1980s when it was realised that examining the geographic locations of a series of crimes could be used to calculate the offender's likely area of residence. Underlying this approach is the "least effort principle". In other words, given two alternative courses of action, people will choose the one that requires least effort and therefore often commit crimes close to home. Geographic profiling is most commonly associated with former Vancouver Detective Kim Rossmo but has also been used by Canter within his suggestion that offenders are either "marauders" or "commuters"—the former strike out from their base, while the latter travel some distance from their base to commit their crimes.

We consider this type of reasoning in the next chapter when we discuss Jack the Ripper.

The Structural Tradition

The structural tradition can be viewed as attempting to answer a different set of questions from those which dominate the medico-psychological tradition. It is less interested in, for example, the micro dynamics of the pathology of individual serial killers and with analysing crime scene patterns, and more concerned with macro questions about which groups most regularly fall victim to serial murder; the periods in history when there were more (or less) serial killers; and which countries seem to produce more serial murderers than others. In essence it champions the idea that wider social forces may drive people in a particular direction even if that direction will be viewed as "pathological" by the majority. This approach can find its roots in the work of the French sociologist Emile Durkheim (1858–1917) who, for example, pointed to a more societal explanation for what had been regarded until then as the individualistic act of suicide.

As with the medico-psychological tradition, there are also a set of assumptions underlying the structural tradition. Chief amongst these is the belief that at any given time there will always be a small number of people (for various reasons) who will want to repeatedly kill. If this reality is constant why should it be only at some times, in some societies, that serial killing becomes an issue? It therefore considers how this small number of offenders gets access to their victims, and how they use that access to create the opportunity to kill. Only then are researchers in this tradition interested in what might have motivated the serial killer to kill. Finally, it is suggested that if we want to reduce the incidence of serial murder, rather than focussing on the pathology of individual serial murderers, we should instead concentrate on what it is that creates the vulnerabilities in the groups that are targeted by this type of offender and ameliorate or eradicate that vulnerability.

The Canadian anthropologist Professor Elliot Leyton (1986) in his seminal book *Hunting Humans: The Rise of the Modern Multiple*

Murderer was perhaps one of the first academics to argue that, in order to understand the phenomenon of serial killing, factors beyond the medico-psychological tradition needed to be analysed. And, using evidence of North American serial killing since the end of the Second World War, his central thesis was that serial murder should be viewed as a form of "homicidal protest" by frustrated members of the upper working-class and lower middle-classes who tend to kill victims from the middle-classes in a period he labels as "Modern"—see *Table 1*. Leyton does acknowledge that: "Occasionally… they (serial killers) continue a metaphor from the earlier era and discipline unruly [sic] prostitutes and runaways" (1986: 297), although he goes on, "Much more commonly… they punish those above them in the system—preying on unambiguously middle-class figures such as university women" (ibid.).

Table 1

Historical Epochs, Serial Killers and their Victims

	Pre-Industrial Era	Industrial Era—1945	Modern
Killer	Aristocratic	Middle-classes (e.g. doctors and teachers)	Upper working/ lower middle-Class (e.g. security guards and computer technicians)
Victim	Peasantry	"Lower Orders" (e.g. prostitutes and housemaids)	Middle-classes (e.g. university students)

Source: Leyton, 1986: 269–295

Leyton argued that during the "Industrial Era", which he roughly placed as starting in the late 19th-century and lasting until the end of the Second World War, was one "in which middle-class functionaries—doctors, teachers, professors, civil servants, who belonged to the class created to serve the needs of the new triumphant bourgeoisie, preyed on members of the lower orders, especially prostitutes and housemaids" (p.276). In this era, Leyton suggests that the crimes of serial killers were a symbolic extension of the need for industrial discipline. In other words, serial killers were taking to their most heinous conclusion the unprecedented control demanded by the cash-nexus of industrial capitalism. Serial killers removed those who lived outside the new moral order, which demanded the maximum extraction of value from the industrial proletariat: "In killing the failures and the unruly renegades from the system ... they acted as enforcers of the new moral order" (p.276).

Widening the analysis — Serial Murder in Britain

Does Leyton's analysis apply to Britain? A number of academics have attempted to consider whether British serial murder should be viewed as a form of "homicidal protest", as described by Leyton, including Chris Grover and Keith Soothill (1997) and David Wilson (2006; 2009). Using Harold Shipman as their example — who largely murdered and some elderly men — Grover and Soothill, for example, suggest that by widening the focus of social relations beyond class relations to include other social relations, such as patriarchy, that it is still possible that "homicidal protest" has some conceptual value in the British context. In their article they suggested that "widening the analysis in this way provides scope for being able to classify a greater variety of serial killers." They also maintain that there is evidence that among some British serial killers a degree of socio-economic frustration may have existed. However, they claimed that it would be both bold and inappropriate to identify socio-economic frustration as either a necessary or sufficient condition for serial killing.

Equally, they claimed that as a result of Leyton's failure to consider social relations other than those of capitalism (and therefore of class), Leyton cannot easily explain why the victims of British serial killers tend to be females, children, young people, gay men and pensioners. In short, they argue that we need to locate serial murder within power relations that go beyond those of class. Only then can "homicidal protest" remain understandable as a form of revenge, but a revenge that is wreaked upon relatively powerless groups in society.

This argument has found support from feminist commentators who have argued with both fervour and conviction that it needs to be recognised that Britain is both a capitalist *and* a patriarchal society. Violence against women and children is thus seen as being reflective of patriarchal relations through which men maintain power over women and children. Hence, recognising patriarchal relations, it becomes clearer as to why serial killers often murder women and children. It is an expression of power through which men are able to dominate and oppress women and children.

Wilson has developed this analysis further. For example he views the murder of gay men and the elderly by serial killers as an extension of the homophobia present in British society and also the more general powerlessness and invisibility of older people in our culture. It is this powerlessness, Wilson argues, that has contributed to this latter group being most regularly attacked by serial murderers, such as Harold Shipman—all of which is discussed more fully in *Chapter Four*. In short the structural tradition has suggested that to truly understand why serial killers kill we need to investigate the very nature of the social structure—the society—that has created these people whom we define and label as serial killers. The answers lie in the social landscape within which serial murder occurs—exploring key social institutions such as the economy, the polity, the family, religion and education is of considerable importance for academics adopting this approach. And, as is implicit in this analysis, it also suggests that the responsibility for serial killing therefore does not lie so much with the individual serial killer, but can be better found within the social and economic structure of the country which does not reward the efforts of all, and in particular has marginalised large sections of society. It therefore should come as no surprise that the victims of British serial killers have been almost exclusively confined to certain marginalised groups in our culture—the elderly, gay men, sex workers, babies and infants, and young people moving home and finding their feet elsewhere in the country, and that women make up a significant number in all but one of these categories.

Revision

- What are the main differences between the medico-psychological and the structural traditions?
- What are the following: the homology assumption; the behavioural consistency hypothesis; and, the least effort principle.
- Name two forms of offender profiling
- What is homicidal protest?

Further Reading

A number of books were cited throughout this chapter and reading these for yourself will allow you to follow the arguments that we have made more closely. For those who would like to pursue the medico-psychological tradition a little more fully, Adrian Raine (2013), *The Anatomy of Violence: The Biological Roots of Crime*, London: Allen Lane offers a comprehensive overview into the history of this particular approach, as well as outlining Raine's own research interests. As for the structural tradition, a good starting point is Grover and Soothill's 1997 article "British Serial Killing: Towards a Structural Explanation" which can be downloaded at http://britsoccrim.org/volume2/008.pdf The article also discusses Leyton's "homicidal protest" at some length. The work of D Wilson (2009)—especially *A History of British Serial Killing*, London: Sphere was cited throughout.

The work of Robert Hare was mentioned in relation to psychopathy. This can be found in Hare (1991), *Manual for the Hare Psychopathy Checklist-Revised*, Toronto: Multi-Health Systems. So too we alluded to the work of David Canter. Professor Canter has recently produced a very useful introduction to forensic psychology see Canter (2010), *Forensic Psychology: A Very Short Introduction*, Oxford: Oxford University Press.

HOW IT ALL BEGAN: JACK THE RIPPER

3

> "When the stolid English go in for a scare they take leave of all moderation and common sense. If nonsense were solid, the nonsense that was talked and written about those murders would sink a Dreadnought."
>
> Sir Robert Anderson, *The Lighter Side of My Official Life* (1910)

Jack the Ripper is not the world's first "serial killer", but he nonetheless retains a stranglehold on the public's imagination. For example, he is by far the most popular subject of the hundred bestselling books in Amazon's criminology list, with such books as: *The Complete History of Jack the Ripper*; *Uncovering Jack the Ripper's London*; *Jack the Ripper: The Facts*; and *Portrait of a Killer: Jack the Ripper—Case Closed* all competing for sales. If you were so inclined you could pay to join a walking tour to "retrace the steps" of the Ripper, visiting the murder sites, the haunts that were frequented, such as the famous pub the Ten Bells in Whitechapel and, in 2006, Jack was even voted the "Worst Briton over the Last 1,000 Years" in a poll conducted for *BBC History* magazine, beating, among others, Titus Oates, King John and Oswald Mosley to the title.

Keying "Jack the Ripper" into Google will produce nearly three million hits, with the most comprehensive link being casebook.org, which claims to be the "world's largest public repository of Ripper-related information". The website's mission statement is written by Stephen P Ryder:

> "In the past 110 years, the name 'Jack the Ripper' has become synonymous with evil and misogyny, eliciting images of foggy nights and

> gas-lit streets in the minds of millions worldwide. The mass media and entertainment industries are largely responsible for the popularity of the subject, but they are also to blame for many of the myths and misconceptions which have crept in among the facts of the case. Sloppy research performed by those motivated by personal dreams of fame and greed has only added to the mire. Though this situation has recently been aided by the valiant efforts of a handful of diligent researchers, the myths persist, the lies are repeated, and the facts of the case remain hidden beneath a cloud of confusion. It is our hope that the information provided by Casebook: Jack the Ripper will help scatter this cloud and, perhaps, finally allow a glimpse into that most elusive aspect of the mystery: the truth."

Sir Robert Anderson, the detective in charge of CID at the time of the murders, might well have appreciated Ryder's attempts to find a way through the "cloud of confusion"—or, as Anderson more bluntly expressed it the "nonsense", that has surrounded the case for over a century. Ryder concludes by imploring readers to "remember that the whole of this fantastic mystery revolves around the deaths of five women whose lives were as precious and as ephemeral as our own... do not ignore their humanity, as the Ripper did, but embrace it. Only then can you truly appreciate the tragedy of the case. Only then can you understand why the search must continue."

In this chapter we will provide some basic material about Jack the Ripper and his victims and, in doing so, we would ask you to begin the process of using that information to assess this serial killer from either the medico-psychological or structural traditions. Use this case study to assess which of these traditions makes more sense when trying to understand this iconic serial killer. Here too remember that criminology is a "rendezvous discipline" and, as such, just as comfortable using historical documents as analysing crime scenes, or interviewing offenders.

Key Term — Rendezvous Discipline

Criminology is a "multi-disciplinary" subject and contains arguments that have been derived from history, philosophy, sociology, psychology, law, genetics, geography and architecture. These various influences "rendezvous" around the subject of crime.

Table 1

Who was Jack the Ripper?—Top 5 Suspects

James Maybrick	Liverpool businessman; died 1889; left diary purporting to be Jack the Ripper.
Francis Tumblety	American known to be in Whitechapel at the time of the murders.
Walter Sickert	Painter favoured by the novelist Patricia Cornwell.
Price Albert Victor	Part of the so-called "Royal Conspiracy" to cover up the killings.
Aaron Kosminski	A Polish Jew living in Whitechapel.

Adapted from casebook.org

To help you come to a conclusion about these questions there are a variety of sources that you can consult. One advantage of the obsessive public interest in Jack the Ripper is that most of the primary sources relating to the so-called Whitechapel Murders (1888-91) have now been collected and are freely available in the public domain. Perhaps the most valuable is *The Ultimate Jack the Ripper Sourcebook: An Illustrated Encyclopaedia* (2000) by Stewart Evans and Keith Skinner. This includes all the Scotland Yard reports, witness statements, press accounts and other Home Office files. Also helpful is Paul Begg's *Jack the Ripper: The Facts* (2004), given that it tries to place the murders within a historical context. Begg states that 85 new books have been published about Jack the Ripper since the centenary of the murders in 1988. Most, if not all, of them have proposed a name for the killer. We will not do so here but for those who are interested, casebook.org lists the main candidates and you can even vote for or nominate your favourite suspect. Table 1 identifies the "Top Five" suspects.

Mary Ann Nichols — The First of the "Canonical Five"

The "Whitechapel Murders" and the crimes committed by Jack the Ripper are often presumed to be one and the same thing. However, the police files on the Whitechapel Murders begin with the murder of Emma Smith on 3/4 April 1888 and end with the murder of Frances Coles on 13 February 1891. In total, eleven murders are included in these files, but how many of them should be attributed to Jack the Ripper? The standard answer to this question is five, starting with the murder of Mary Ann Nichols on 31 August 1888, then: Annie Chapman on 8 September; Elizabeth Stride and Catherine Eddowes in the early hours of 30 September; and finally Mary Jane Kelly on 9 November. Jack the Ripper therefore fits our definition of a serial killer: he killed three or more victims in a period greater than 30 days.

Most Ripper scholars attribute only five rather than all eleven victims to him because of a confidential memorandum written by Sir Melville Macnaghten in February 1894. Macnaghten, who had joined the Metropolitan Police Force as Assistant Chief Constable CID in June 1889, wrote this memo in response to a newspaper claim that Jack the Ripper was a recently detained lunatic called Thomas Hayne Cutbush. In it, Macnaghten states unequivocally that "the Whitechapel murderer had five victims — & 5 victims only". He then names the "canonical five" and expressly dismisses, for example, Martha Tabram who is sometimes thought of as a Ripper victim. This is an important document because, although Macnaghten joined the Met after the Ripper murders had ended, he was in a good position to know the intricacies of the investigation. So any comments he made on the case must carry authority.

The first of the "canonical five" is Mary Ann Nichols was also known as "Polly". She was born on 26 August 1845 to Edward Nichols, a locksmith, and his wife Caroline, who worked as a laundress. The family lived in Shoe Lane, off Fleet Street. In January 1864 Mary Ann married an Oxford-born printer called William Nichols at St Bride's Parish Church in Fleet Street, and between 1866 and 1879 they had five children. While this indicates that their marriage was publicly fruitful, it was also privately stormy, and it broke down completely one year later. William suggested that this was a result of Mary Ann's alcoholism, but her father denied that she was a heavy drinker, suggesting instead that the marriage failed as a result of William having an affair with the nurse who looked after Mary Ann during her last pregnancy. Whatever the truth, Mary Ann moved out of the family home in September 1880 and went to live in the Lambeth Workhouse, where she stayed for some nine months, and where she would return periodically over the next eight years.

At first, after their separation, William continued to support Mary Ann, but he eventually stopped the payments. When the parish authorities tried to collect more maintenance money from him, he explained that his wife had deserted her children, taken up with another man, and was now earning her living as a prostitute. He won the case, and at the time of her death he had not seen Mary Ann for three years.

Between April and July 1888, Mary Ann worked as a domestic servant in the home of a teetotal couple—Mr and Mrs Cowdry—who lived in Wandsworth, a job found for her by the matron of the Lambeth Workhouse. It is logical to presume that the matron had deliberately placed Mary Ann in a situation where she would not have access to alcohol, but unfortunately this plan backfired. On 12 July Mrs Cowdry sent Mary Ann's father a postcard to say that she had stolen clothing worth £3 10s. and absconded. At the time of her death, Mary Ann was living in a doss house, known as the White House, in Flower and Dean Street, where men and women were allowed to sleep together.

Mary Ann was five feet two inches tall, with a dark complexion, brown eyes, brown, greying hair, high cheekbones and discoloured teeth. Her associates viewed her as a very clean woman who tried to keep herself to herself and rarely talked about her affairs. This might suggest something of the regret she must have felt for the children she had left behind. On the night that she died she went out drinking in the Frying Pan in Brick Lane, but by 1.20 a.m. she was in a lodging house in Thrawl Street, where she was asked for fourpence for her bed. She did not have the money so was turned out. In all likelihood, then, she was murdered while trying to earn enough cash simply to secure a bed for the night.

Later, Mary Ann was spotted by Mrs Emily Holland, with whom she had once shared a room in Thrawl Street. Emily described her former roommate as drunk and said she found her slumped against the wall of a grocer's shop. According to her statement, Emily tried to persuade Mary Ann to go home with her, but Mary Ann wanted to earn her doss money, so she staggered up Whitechapel Road and into Buck's Row—known today as Durward Street—where she met her death.

Mary Ann was found with two bruises on her face, one on each side. There were two cuts to her throat—one four inches long, the other eight inches—both of which were so deep as to reach the vertebrae of her neck. There was also bruising on her abdomen, and on her right side three or four cuts running downwards—a contemporary account claims that the "lower part of the person was completely ripped open". All of the wounds had been inflicted with a sharp knife. While not commented upon by the coroner, several newspapers reported that Mary Ann might have been wearing a ring, which had been removed by the killer.

It would seem fair to conclude that Mary Ann turned her back to her murderer—possibly intending to have intercourse in this position—and that this gave him the opportunity to cut her throat. Cutting his victim's throat would also have left her unable to scream, allowing him more time to mutilate his dying victim. This suggests that Jack the Ripper was "act focused"—he wanted to kill his victims quickly—and was not interested in prolonging the process by which they died. He sought a dead victim, so thereafter he could feed his fantasies with an inert body.

Paul Begg notes that all of the murders (with the exception of Elizabeth Stride's, when the Ripper was disturbed) were "characterised by extensive mutilation of the victim, the womb being the target of his attacks". Dr Llewellyn, who conducted the full post-mortem examination on Mary Ann, thought that her killer must have had at least some, albeit crude, anatomical knowledge. His opinion has been used as supporting evidence by many of those who propose doctors or people with a medical background as the murderer. Finally, there is no evidence that the killer engaged in sex with Mary Ann, or indeed with any of his future victims.

Four More Murders

There is a striking degree of similarity between the five victims: they all worked as prostitutes, all had problems with alcohol, and they were all—with the exception of Mary Jane Kelly—in their forties (see *Table 2*). Annie Chapman, the second victim, was born Annie Smith in September of either 1840 or 1841. Her father, George, was a soldier in the Life Guards. Annie's first job seems to have been as a domestic servant, and in May 1869 she married a coachman named John Chapman. Together they had three children, but Annie drank heavily and her "dissolute habits" eventually led to the couple's separation in 1882. She was given an allowance of ten shillings a week by her ex-husband, but when he died in 1886 that came to an abrupt end. Thereafter, Annie drifted from one relationship to another, and she tried to support herself by selling matches and flowers bought at Stratford Market. Her friends described her at the time of her murder as "addicted to drink". However, it was only when her ex-husband died that she was forced into prostitution, which reveals the precarious nature of life in late-Victorian England for working-class women.

On the night of her murder Annie had been drinking in the Britannia public house on the corner of Dorset Street, near where she had been staying at a lodging house. She returned to her lodgings, and, like Mary Ann Nichols, was asked for money for her bed. She did not have it but told the warden—Tim Donovan—that he should not let out her bed because she would return soon enough with the cash. Donovan stated that Annie was drunk but was walking straight. There were also some unsubstantiated reports that she went on to the Ten Bells pub on the corner of Fournier Street. In any event, Annie was found dead, lying on her back, in the rear yard of 29 Hanbury Street. Her throat had been cut through to the spine, and a portion of her small intestine and abdomen was lying on the ground over her right shoulder, but still attached to her body. Begg describes the remainder of her injuries: "from the pelvis the uterus and its appendages, with the upper portion of the vagina and the posterior two-thirds of the bladder, had been entirely removed".

Table 2

Five murders

Name	Age	Occupation	Time	Place	Alcoholic
Mary Ann Nichols	43	Prostitute	Friday 0230	Street	Yes
Annie Chapman	48	Prostitute	Saturday 0600	Street	Yes
Elizabeth Stride	44	Prostitute	Sunday 0100	Street	Yes
Catherine Eddowes	46	Prostitute	Sunday 0145	Street	Yes
Mary Jane Kelly	24	Prostitute	Friday "Early morning"	House	Yes

Adapted from Wilson (2009) *A History of British Serial Killing*

Elizabeth Stride and Catherine Eddowes were killed just over three weeks later, on the same night. This is often described as the "double event", a phrase used in a postcard purportedly written by Jack the Ripper on 1 October 1888. Elizabeth was murdered first; then, just 45 minutes later, Catherine was killed. Their murders are of particular significance because both seem to have been witnessed.

Elizabeth Gustafsdotter was born in Sweden in November 1843. She emigrated to London in February 1867, after inheriting 65 Swedish krona from her mother's estate. This seems to have been an attempt to put the past behind her, as she had already been arrested by the Swedish police for prostitution. She married a carpenter named John Stride in March 1869, and soon they were running a coffee shop together. However, John suffered ill-health, and in January 1879 Elizabeth asked the Swedish Church in London for financial assistance. John was admitted to Poplar Workhouse in August 1884 before being sent to the Poplar and Stepney Sick Asylum, where he died of heart disease two months later.

The Strides' marriage seems to have broken down three years before John's death, with Elizabeth's heavy drinking reportedly the principal cause. She spent time in the Whitechapel Workhouse infirmary, and would eventually be sentenced to seven days' hard labour for being drunk and disorderly and soliciting on 13 November 1884. She liked to tell people that her husband and two of her children had died in a shipping accident in 1878, and Cornwell notes that Elizabeth had "led a life of lies, most of them pitiful attempts to weave a brighter, more dramatic tale than the truth of her depressing, desperate life". Begg suggests that she might also have masqueraded as another woman, Elizabeth Watts, and she certainly had a variety of nicknames, among them Long Liz, Hippy Lip Annie and Mother Gum.

After the collapse of her marriage, Elizabeth lived on and off with a man named Michael Kidney. By all accounts it was a stormy relationship, with Elizabeth disappearing for days or weeks at a time: "It was the drink that made her go away," claimed Kidney after Elizabeth's death. Support for this statement comes in the form of the numerous appearances that Elizabeth made before the magistrates. For example, she was charged in February and October 1887 and February and September 1888 with being drunk and disorderly and using obscene language. Kidney and Elizabeth parted company for the last time on 25 September—just five days before her death. As a result, he was initially suspected of her murder.

Elizabeth was seen drinking in the Bricklayer's Arms in Settles Street on the night of her death, and she may have been sold a bunch of grapes by one Matthew Packer between 11 p.m. and midnight, although none were found in her stomach during her post-mortem. Her body was discovered in a passageway beside 40 Berner Street, which had been converted into the International Working Men's Educational Club. That night about a hundred people had turned up at the club to debate "Why Jews Should Be Socialists", with most not leaving before 11.30 p.m. Several others stayed on to drink until well after midnight. Clearly, then, people must have been around when Elizabeth was attacked on Berner Street. In particular, Israel Schwartz followed a man into the street from Commercial Road. He saw the figure approach Elizabeth—who was standing outside the gates of the club—stop, exchange a few words with her and then assault her. Schwartz thought it was a domestic dispute, so he crossed the street to avoid becoming involved. He then saw a second man leave a pub on the corner and light his pipe. Next he heard someone shout "Lipski"—a reference to a notorious Jewish murderer who had been hanged the previous year, which might have been intended to scare off Schwartz. He did indeed run away—as did the man with the pipe—but he reported all he had witnessed the following day at Leman Street police station.

If Schwartz is to be believed, he undoubtedly saw the man who murdered Elizabeth Stride, and he provided the police with a description of Jack the Ripper. More immediately, because of Schwartz's presence and/or the man with the pipe, or possibly due to the arrival several minutes later of Louis Diemshutz, who worked at the club as a steward, this time the killer did not linger over his victim's body. He cut Elizabeth's throat, but her body was not mutilated in any way. Unfortunately for Catherine Eddowes, that meant the killer had unfinished business that night.

Catherine Eddowes—also known as Kate Kelly—was born in Wolverhampton on 14 April 1842. Her father was a tinplate worker and her mother a cook, and the family moved to London when Catherine was just one year old. Nevertheless, she spent some of her childhood back in Wolverhampton, and she would eventually find work there as a tinplate stamper. However, she was fired from that job and ran off to Birmingham, where she stayed with an uncle who made boots and shoes. Again, though, this did not work out, so she returned to Wolverhampton in 1861, where she met and set up home with a former soldier called Thomas Quinn. The couple had a son, moved to London, and then three further children were born. However, Catherine's heavy drinking and fiery temperament had destroyed the relationship by 1880, when she turned to prostitution. She moved into a lodging house called Cooney's in Flower and Dean Street, where she met John Kelly. He denied that Catherine was involved in prostitution, but admitted that she sometimes drank to excess—she was charged with being drunk and disorderly in September 1881.

On the day of her death, Catherine had again been drinking heavily enough to be arrested by PC Louis Robinson at 8.30 p.m. She was taken to Bishopsgate police station to "sleep it off". Just before one o'clock the following morning the station sergeant asked PC George Hutt to check if anyone could be released. By this time Catherine was sober, so she was freed by Hutt, who asked her to shut the station door on her way out. "All right. Good night, old cock," she said as she walked into the early hours of the morning, just as Elizabeth Stride's body was being found.

Catherine seems to have gone in the opposite direction to Flower and Dean Street, and eventually she must have wandered into Mitre Square, where her body was found. By all accounts, the square was poorly lit, but the patrolling PC Watkins reported nothing unusual at 1.30 a.m., when he was on his rounds. However, just five minutes later, a commercial traveller in the cigarette business named Joseph

Lawende noticed a couple standing at the entrance of a passageway leading to the square. Lawende described a woman wearing clothes that matched those worn by Catherine that night. Strangely, at the inquest into Catherine's death he did not give a description of the man who was with her, but *The Times* provided a brief pen picture, and the Home Office files contain a full description that can only have come from Lawende. Perhaps the police were trying to keep Lawende's information out of the public domain in the hope of using the intelligence he provided to trap the killer.

In any event, Catherine's body was discovered by PC Watkins when he returned to Mitre Square on his beat at 1.45 a.m. As he was later to tell the *Star* newspaper, Catherine had been "ripped up like a pig in the market... I have been in the force a long while, but I never saw such a sight." The attack had been ferocious: her throat had been cut; after death her killer had mutilated her face and abdomen; her intestines had been cut out and placed over her right shoulder; and her left kidney and uterus had been removed. The damage to Catherine's face—the tip of her nose and her ear lobes had been cut off, and her cheeks slashed—was clearly deliberate. As Cornwell observes: "the face is the person. To mutilate it is personal."

A search was made of the area near where Catherine's body was discovered and some graffiti was found. Again, this has become part of Jack the Ripper folklore. It reportedly read, "the Jews are the men that will not be blamed for nothing", but there is no way of knowing if it was connected to the murders or had been in existence for some time.

The last of the "canonical five" was Mary Jane Kelly, also known as "Black Mary", "Ginger" and "Marie Jeanette Kelly". By far the youngest of the victims, her body was found at 13 Miller's Court, Dorset Street. Her murder was unusual because she was not murdered in public, and the extensive injuries inflicted upon her indicate that the killer was able to spend some considerable time with Mary Jane's body after her death. More than any of the other murders, this one represents the ultimate expression of Jack the Ripper's hatred of his female victims. By the time of her death, Mary Jane would have been all too aware that there was a killer walking the streets of Whitechapel murdering prostitutes. However, she continued to sell sexual services, a simple fact that highlights the desperation of the young women who were involved in the sex industry in late-Victorian Britain.

Mary Jane was born in Limerick, Ireland, she had spent some of her childhood in Wales, and at 16 had married a mineworker who was killed three years later in an explosion. After this tragedy she moved to Cardiff, where she first seems to have become involved in prostitution. Eventually she made her way to London. By April 1887, she was in a relationship with a porter called Joseph Barnett, but at the time of her murder their relationship had begun to cool, perhaps because Barnett disapproved of her work as a prostitute. As a result, Barnett lived apart from Mary Jane, who was renting a room in Miller's Court from a well-known East End pimp called John McCarthy.

There are several conflicting witness testimonies relating to when Mary Jane was last seen alive, and with whom she was seen entering Miller's Court. But there is no doubt about what happened to her after her death, with the police taking photographs of both Mary Jane's body and the interior and exterior of 13 Miller's Court. Her ears, nose, cheeks and eyebrows had been partly removed. Dr Thomas Bond—who conducted Mary Jane's preliminary post-mortem at the crime scene—described the state of her body:

> "The legs were wide apart, the left thigh at right angles to the trunk & the right forming an obtuse angle with the pubes. The whole surface of the abdomen & thighs was removed & the abdominal cavity emptied of its viscera. The breasts were cut off, the arms mutilated by several jagged wounds & the face hacked beyond recognition of the features...the viscera were found in various parts viz; the uterus & kidneys with one breast under the head, the other breast by the right foot, the liver between the feet, the intestines by the right side & the spleen by the left side of the body. The flaps removed from the

> abdomen & thighs were on a table ... the Pericardium was open below & the Heart absent.

When Mary Jane was buried ten days later at Shoreditch Church there were three large wreaths on her coffin, two crowns of artificial flowers and a cross that bore the words: "A last tribute of respect to Mary Kelly. May she rest in peace, and may her murderer be brought to justice."

Jack the Ripper — A profile

Today, if the police were faced with a series of murders such as those that have just been described, they would have access to a wealth of forensic expertise that was not available to their Victorian counterparts. There would be a mass of DNA evidence available for analysis, fingerprints, CCTV camera footage, and mobile phone records. The police might also call upon profilers, who would suggest that the characteristics of the murderer could be deduced from a carefully considered examination of his offences. In particular, a profiler would look closely at five areas: the crime scene; the nature of the attacks; forensic evidence; a medical examination of the victim; and finally the victim's characteristics.

Based on this type of analysis, as we have discussed in *Chapter Two*, conclusions might be drawn as to whether Jack the Ripper was "organized" or "disorganized" and, on that basis, some assumptions made about his personality. In the case of Jack the Ripper it might also be noted that there was no evidence of sexual assault and that he was "act focused"—all of his victims were killed quickly. He did not torture them while they were alive but, when he had time to be alone with a dead victim, he mutilated her abdomen and sometimes her face. He removed body parts, and sometimes took other "trophies", such as Mary Ann Nichols's ring. Obviously, the attacks on the abdomens of his victims have sexual overtones, but we might speculate whether Jack the Ripper was sexually competent, and perhaps therefore single. While he murdered women who sold sexual services, his choice of victim does not seem to have stemmed from a desire to buy those services. Rather, prostitutes, unlike most women at the time, would simply allow him to get sufficiently close to commit his crimes.

It is interesting that Jack the Ripper committed most of his murders in the street, which meant that he usually did not have much of an opportunity to be alone with his dead victims before being disturbed by passers-by. This meant he only fully accomplished his goal in the case of his final victim, Mary Jane Kelly, whom he murdered indoors and so was able to mutilate at his leisure. He also never seemed to give much thought to his escape route, or indeed how he would dispose of his victim's body. All of this suggests that he was a disorganized killer, who had no plan and merely sought out any random opportunity to kill. When he did have the time to be alone with Mary Jane Kelly, the mutilation of her body was so comprehensive that her identity was virtually obliterated.

The timing of his attacks would also seem to have been significant. They always occurred in the early hours of the morning on a Friday, Saturday or Sunday. This would seem to indicate that he had some form of unskilled work that occupied him during the week, and that the opportunity to be alone—that is, away from those who knew him, were related to him, or were living with him—came only during the weekend. All of the attacks also occurred in a very narrow geographical area, which strongly suggests that he lived locally—he was too disorganized to travel any great distance. Based on the "least effort principle" it would seem reasonable to assume that he had lodgings near to Buck's Row, where his first victim, Mary Ann Nichols, was killed. In short, he was a "marauder" rather than a "commuter". He surely had somewhere to return to after each attack, where could clean himself and perhaps hide while the police conducted house-to-house searches.

Given all of this, a profiler might suggest that Jack the Ripper was a white man of limited intelligence and education, under the age of 45 and living in Whitechapel. From the nature of his offences, it seems highly unlikely that he would have been interested in writing letters to the press. There is also no real evidence of any medical training or surgical knowledge in his crimes; rather, he seems to have been curious about female internal organs. Finally, the nature of the murders he committed suggests that he was insane.

Eyewitness Testimony

At least two people saw Jack the Ripper and provided descriptions to the police: Israel Schwartz, who saw Elizabeth Stride being assaulted in Berner Street; and Joseph Lawende, who spotted Catherine Eddowes with her killer in Mitre Square. Their descriptions are remarkably similar. Schwartz recalled seeing a short, stocky, 30-year-old with a moustache who was wearing a black cap with a peak. *The Times* reported that Lawende witnessed a man of shabby appearance, about 30-years-of-age, five feet nine inches tall, with a fair complexion and a small moustache, wearing a peaked grey cloth cap. The Home Office files relating to Lawende's description go into more detail (and knock a couple of inches off the height, bringing it more in line with Schwartz's description): "aged about thirty, five foot seven or eight, of fair complexion, with a fair moustache, of medium build, wearing a pepper-and-salt-coloured loose jacket, a grey cloth cap with peak of the same colour, and a reddish handkerchief tied in a knot around the neck, and having the appearance of a sailor".

Sir Robert Anderson outlined where the police's attention was focused in light of these descriptions:

> "One did not need to be a Sherlock Holmes to discover that the criminal was a sexual maniac of a virulent type; that he was living in the immediate vicinity of the scenes of the murders; and that, if he was not living absolutely alone, his people knew of his guilt, and refused to give him up to justice. During my absence abroad the Police had made a house-to-house search for him, investigating the case of every man in the district whose circumstances were such that he could go and come and get rid of bloodstains in secret. And the conclusion we came to was that he and his people were certain low-class Polish Jews; for it is a remarkable fact that people of that class in the East End will not give up one of their number to Gentile justice.

When his book was published, Anderson was criticised for the anti-Semitism of this passage, and he had to justify his observations in various contemporary newspapers and magazines. However, amid the controversy, an even more significant passage was largely overlooked, both at the time and for the next 77 years: "the only person who had ever had a good view of the murderer unhesitatingly identified the suspect the instant he was confronted with him; but he refused to give evidence against him".

In 1987 the so-called "Swanson marginalia" were discovered and received considerable publicity in the *Daily Telegraph.* Chief Inspector Donald Swanson was placed in overall charge of the Whitechapel Murders inquiry in September 1888. He retired in 1903 but kept in touch with his former colleague, Sir Robert Anderson, who later gave Swanson a presentation copy of his memoirs. At some point Swanson made a series of pencil comments in the margins, but of specific interest are those appended to the section quoted above, where he has written: "and after this identification which suspect knew, no other murder of this kind took place in London". He also notes that "this identification" took place at the "Seaside Home where he had been sent by us with great difficulty in order to subject him to identification, and he knew he was identified".

The "Seaside Home" is now presumed to be the Convalescent Police Seaside Home in Hove, which was opened in 1890. It seems that the police had a suspect and forced him to visit Hove, where he was officially identified, presumably by either Lawende or Schwartz. Swanson claims that this confrontation put an end to the murders because thereafter the suspect knew that he would be watched closely by the police. Further details are then given in the marginalia: "in a very short time the suspect with his hands tied behind his back, he was sent to Stepney Workhouse and then to Colney Hatch and died shortly afterwards—Kosminski was the suspect—DSS". Of course, if this is true, it answers a question that is often raised about Jack the Ripper: as he was never caught, why did the murders not continue into the 1890s?

The identification of Kosminski (no first name is given) brings us back to the confidential Macnaghten memorandum. In this, Macnaghten first states that "no one ever saw the Whitechapel murderer" (which, of course, contradicts what has just been described), but then he mentions three people, "any one of whom would have been more likely than Cutbush to have committed this series of murders": Montague Druitt, whom he wrongly describes as a doctor (he was a barrister), Kosminski (like Swanson, Macnaghten does not include a first name) and Michael Ostrog.

A generation of research has been able to demonstrate conclusively that neither Montague Druitt nor Michael Ostrog could have been Jack the Ripper. For example, although Druitt committed suicide in late-1888 and was in all likelihood insane, he seems to have taken his own life after being sacked from a teaching job at a school in Blackheath for sexual impropriety. While these two issues do make him an interesting suspect, research by Paul Begg has demonstrated that Druitt was playing cricket on the day after Mary Ann Nichols was murdered and ten days after Mary Jane Kelly was killed he was present at a board meeting of his cricket club. Whatever caused Druitt to take his own life—most probably in early December 1888, it seems unlikely to have been the result of his having been Jack the Ripper. Meanwhile, Ostrog was a career criminal who spent most of his life in prison for a series of opportunistic thefts. Nothing in his record suggests that he could display the type of violence that was perpetrated against the Ripper's victims, and Begg goes as far as to say that the "mystery is why anyone ever thought that he might have been [Jack the Ripper]".

Macnagthen describes Kosminski as "a Polish Jew, & resident in Whitechapel. This man became insane owing to many years indulgence in solitary vices. He had a great hatred of women, especially of the prostitute class, & had strong homicidal tendencies; he was removed to a lunatic asylum about March 1889. There were many circs [*sic*] connected with this man which made him a strong suspect."

Two primary sources—Anderson's autobiography and Swanson's marginalia—provide us with details about someone they strongly suspected of being Jack the Ripper. Allied to these we also have Macnaghten's memorandum. In effect, all three tell the same story: a Polish Jew living in the heart of the murder area who had people to look after him was responsible for the murders, and he was eventually committed to an asylum on account of his "solitary vices" by his family in 1889. A thorough search of asylum records by the author Martin Fido (2001) unearthed only one Kosminski who was admitted at this time—a young man named Aaron—and no other Kosminski has ever been located. So it is likely—although not certain—that this was Anderson and Swanson's suspect, even though some of the details that each provides are at odds with what we know from historical records.

The Structural Tradition and Jack the Ripper

While we can never be certain of the identity of Jack the Ripper, we do know the identities of his victims. Their stories reveal much about the precarious life that working-class women led in late Victorian England, and how easy it was for them to slip from relative comfort to abject squalor. For example, the lives of Mary Ann Nichols and Annie Chapman turned when maintenance payments from their former husbands stopped. Their lives—and those of the Ripper's other three victims—became dominated by the need to earn fourpence for a bed for the night, a task made all the more difficult by their addiction to alcohol. This latter dependence also often brought them into contact with the police and Catherine Eddowes, for example, was released from the local station just before her murder. All of the "canonical five" were problem drinkers, and some may have been alcoholics. Selling sexual services provided them with the means to keep their bodies and souls together, and with just enough to buy more alcohol. Their desperation was such that four of them kept working the streets even when they knew there was a killer on the loose.

Five women's need to make money to feed an addiction made them enormously vulnerable to attack by a ruthless serial killer. This is a regular pattern when dealing with British serial killers.

Alcohol would eventually be replaced by heroin and crack, but the simple need to earn enough cash for the next drink or fix creates a sad and desperate connection between those who died at the hands of the Ripper and those who would become victims in the years that followed.

Revision

- What is the basis for attributing just five victims to Jack the Ripper?
- How does the murder of Mary Jane Kelly differ from the murders of the other four victims in the "canonical five"?
- Why is Aaron Kosminski considered a suspect?

Further Reading

Those students who wish to study Jack the Ripper further will find Stewart Evans and Keith Skinner's (2000), *The Ultimate Jack the Ripper Sourcebook* (London: Robinson) a very useful introduction, where they can consult primary sources for themselves. These sources include the Macnaghten memorandum, which is discussed in the chapter. Laurence Alison (ed.) (2005), *The Forensic Psychologist's Casebook: Psychological Profiling and Criminal Investigation* includes a chapter by J Ogan and L Alison called "Jack the Ripper and the Whitechapel Murders: A Very Victorian Critical Incident" which is also worth consulting.

4 AN OVERVIEW OF BRITISH SERIAL MURDER

"Those who cannot remember the past are condemned to repeat it."

George Santayana (1863–1952)

In this chapter we set out a broad outline of serial murder in Britain. In doing so we can begin to develop a more critical understanding of the phenomenon of serial murder and, through that understanding, at the very least, identify patterns or trends that should be of interest to criminologists. For example, is serial killing becoming more common? When was the "high point" of British serial killing? Which groups tend to be targeted by British serial killers? And, are there any significant periods in our history when we had no serial killers? In this chapter we will also concentrate on the absence of serial murder in the "inter-war" years between 1918 and 1939 and ask you to reflect on what that fact might tell us about serial murder more recently.

We have some immediate issues and caveats to the overview that we present. For example, we have chosen as our starting point 1888. However, Jack the Ripper was not our first serial killer and so, in *Chapter Eight*, for example, we discuss the case of another and earlier Victorian serial killer called Mary Ann Cotton. Choosing 1888 as the starting point for this overview is therefore a matter of judgement—a judgement formed in part both by acknowledging that most students believe that serial murder begins with Jack the Ripper and accepting that it is certainly true that it was this case that brought the phenomenon of serial murder to widespread public attention. Mary Ann Cotton's case did not generate the same level of national, public interest as Jack the Ripper and this is in itself an interesting issue to consider.

Even further back in our history we might have started with the commercially driven murders of 16 people in Edinburgh by William Burke and William Hare in 1828 (they killed people so that they could sell the bodies of their victims to anatomists at Edinburgh Medical School) and the activities of their English imitators John Bishop and Thomas Williams, who confessed to five killings in London. However, given that the motivation for these murders was extrinsic rather than intrinsic to the psychology of the murderer we have chosen to ignore them.

Key Term — Intrinsic/Extrinsic Motivation

Extrinsic motivation arises from outside of the individual. The individual engages in behaviour or an activity to gain a reward or avoid punishment. On the other hand *intrinsic* motivation comes from within the individual, who engages in an activity or behaviour because they find it personally satisfying.

The second issue to bear in mind as you read this chapter is that we have included in our overview only those killers who fit with our academic definition of having killed three or more victims in a period of greater than 30 days. This immediately rules out the cases of well-known, British "spree killers" such as Michael Ryan at Hungerford in August 1987, who shot and killed 16 people; Thomas Hamilton at Dunblane, who shot and killed 16 children and their schoolteacher in March 1996; and Derrick Bird who shot and killed 12 people in Whitehaven in June 2010.

You should also note that we have included only those who were tried and convicted at court for murdering three or more victims and have in the main only counted the victims that formed part of the court case against them. We have therefore excluded murderers who were charged, arrested and convicted of one or two murders, even if there are strong suspicions that they killed many more people.

There are two exceptions to these general rules: Harold Shipman was convicted at his trial of murdering 15 people, but a subsequent public inquiry held him responsible for the deaths of 215 in total, so this is the figure that we use throughout; and John Haigh was convicted for a single murder but was undoubtedly responsible for five others, so we have set his total at six. The inquiry into Shipman's activities raised suspicions that he might have committed a total of 260 murders, but as the extra 45 could not be proved we have not included them in our analysis. Similarly, it is often suggested that Dennis Nilsen, Peter Sutcliffe, Robert Black and the Wests committed more murders than are generally attributed to them, but we have included only the murders for which they were convicted at court.

Spates of murders can sometimes also be attributed to a single killer but, for any number of different reasons, that killer is never caught. It is generally assumed, for example, that Patricia Docker, Jemima McDonald and Helen Puttock were all murdered by the same man—nicknamed 'Bible John' by the press—in Glasgow in the late-1960s, but as he was never apprehended we have neither included "Bible John" or his three suspected victims in our overview. So too, in London, eight sex workers were murdered between 1959 and 1965 and their deaths were attributed to a man known in the media as "Jack the Stripper", although this case has never been solved. We have also excluded this case and we have only bent our own rule to include Jack the Ripper because he and his crimes are the foundations of the phenomenon that is at the heart of the book.

Further exclusions come from cases where a series of murders has taken place that is widely assumed to be the work of a serial killer, but when the killer is caught he is charged and convicted of only one crime. For example, Raymond Morris was convicted of the murder of seven-year-old Christine Darby in 1968, but he is suspected of having murdered two other young girls, Diane Tift and Margaret Reynolds. Similarly, we have excluded Paul Brumfitt, who was convicted of murdering two men in 1979 and served 15 years for those crimes. Having been released, he murdered again in February 1999. While cumulatively he murdered enough people to be considered a serial killer, the gap between the second and third murders is simply too great for Brumfitt to be categorised in such a way. Finally, as with the case of Michael Lupo, an Italian who killed four men between 15 March and 18 April 1986 in London, we have excluded any serial killers who were not born or raised in Britain. Nor have we included British serial killers who committed their crimes overseas, such as John Scripps, who murdered three people in Singapore and Thailand and has the dubious distinction of being the last person to be hanged in Singapore, in April 1996.

We have chosen these parameters with some care and have explained our reasoning for doing so. In this way we are attempting to bring some academic rigour to your study of the phenomenon of serial murder, as opposed to the more popular interest that has existed about this subject. We set out in *Table 1* below the 30 killers and their 374 victims who form the basis of our overview, although you should feel free to add to this table when new cases arise.

Table 1

An Overview of British Serial Murder, 1888-Present

Name	Convicted	Occupation	Victims	Number
"Jack the Ripper"	N/A	N/K	Sex workers	5
Thomas Neill Cream	1891	Doctor	Sex workers	3
George Chapman	1903	Publican	Women	3
George Smith	1916	Petty criminal	Women	3
John Haigh	1949	Businessman	Random	6
John Christie	1953	Clerk	Women	7

Name	Convicted	Occupation	Victims	Number
Peter Manuel	1958	Petty criminal	Random	8
Michael Copeland	1965	Soldier	Young person/ gay men	3
Brady/Hindley	1966	Clerk/typist	Children/young people	5
Patrick Mackay	1975	Gardener	Elderly women/ priest	3
Donald Neilson	1976	Builder	Men/young person	3
Trevor Hardy **Hall/Kitto**	1977 1978	Petty criminal Butler/ unemployed	Young women acquaintances/ employer	3 5
Peter Dinsdale	1981	Unemployed	Random	26
Peter Sutcliffe	1981	Lorry Driver	Women/sex workers	13
Dennis Nilsen	1983	Civil servant	Gay men	15
Duffy/Mulcahy	1988	Unemployed	Women/young person	3
Kenneth Erskine	1988	Unemployed	Elderly	7
Beverly Allitt	1993	Nurse	Children	4
Colin Ireland	1993	Unemployed	Gay men	5
Robert Black	1994	Van driver	Children	3

Name	Convicted	Occupation	Victims	Number
Fred/Rose West	1995	Builder/ housewife[1]	Young people/ family member	10
Peter Moore	1996	Cinema owner	Gay men/ random[2]	4
Harold Shipman	2000	Doctor	Elderly	215
Mark Martin[3]	2006	Unemployed	Women	3
Steve Wright	2007	Van Driver	Sex workers	5
Colin Norris	2008	Nurse	Elderly	4

1. Rose West might also be described as a "part-time prostitute".
2. One of Moore's victims was a security guard on a building site that Moore simply chanced upon.
3. Martin killed two of his victims in the company of two other men—Dean Carr and John Ashley.

Some General Observations

There are a number of general points to make about this table. First, and in keeping with what we have described as the structural tradition, the victims of British serial killers are clearly drawn from certain groups: the elderly, gay men, babies and infants, young people moving away from home, and sex workers. Why are these groups so vulnerable to attack? Of course there are overlaps between these general categorisations and so, for example, the description "the elderly" masks the fact that many of the elderly in question were elderly women, rather than elderly men. So too "young person/people" is a very broad description, although it is being employed here so as to capture those young people—as opposed to babies and infants—who have by and large left home and are attempting, for various reasons, to make their own way in the world. Here too there is a gender imbalance, but while some serial killers, such as the Wests concentrated their efforts on young women, others, like Dennis Nilsen were more interested in young men.

Secondly, gay men have been regular targets of serial killers, especially in the latter part of our timeframe—despite the fact that civil partnerships and now marriage have become common and therefore gay relationships are far more open. Perhaps this suggests something about the persistence of homophobia at a time when homosexuality is no longer illegal. It is also worth noting here that whilst two of the serial killers are open about their sexuality—Peter Moore and Dennis Nilsen—we do not know if Michael was gay. Colin Ireland suggested that he chose to kill gay men only because they were vulnerable to attack and therefore suitable targets which would allow him to achieve his objective of becoming famous through their serial murder.

The elderly are the group that has been attacked most regularly by British serial killers. Some 225 elderly people have been murdered by serial killers—a figure that constitutes just over 60 per cent of the total number of victims since 1888. This should make us question the place of the elderly in late modernity, although this has yet to happen despite the awful reality of the Shipman murders. Finally, we should consider absences. For example, there are no Asian, or black British serial killers and, with the exceptions of Myra Hindley, Beverly Allitt and Rosemary West (two of whom killed in conjunction with male partners in a *folie à deux*), all of the British serial killers mentioned here are male.

It is also interesting to note when the serial killers that we have identified were active—see *Table 2* below. To help us chart the peaks and troughs in the activities of serial killers we have divided our sample further into four distinct phases—*Victorian/Pre-War; Inter-War; Post War;* and *Thatcher/Consensus*—which roughly corresponds to the periods *1888–1914; 1915–1945; 1946–1978;* and finally *1979-to the present day*. The first phase produced three serial killers and eleven victims, while the last has produced 14 serial killers and 263 victims, despite the fact that these phases are roughly comparable in terms of time.

Table 2

Victorian/ Pre-war	Inter-war	Post-war	Thatcher/Consensus
1888–1914	1915–1945	1946–1978	1979-present day
3 serial killers/11 victims	1 serial killer/3 victims	11 serial killers/43 victims	14 serial killers/263 victims

Statistically 1986 emerges as one of the most interesting years, as it was then that the greatest numbers of serial killers are known to have been active. It was during this year, for example, that Duffy and Mulcahy murdered their three victims; Kenneth Erskine murdered seven; Robert Black murdered ten-year-old Sarah Harper; and Harold Shipman murdered eight people in 1986. Indeed if we had included Lupo's victims in this graph the number of serial killers active in Britain in this year would have been six, compared to an average over our time frame of two per year. Finally, whilst there are relatively few numbers of victims between 1960–1972 and between 1999–2014, we can see that the numbers of victims and the numbers of serial killers increases over our timeframe.

A History Lesson — The British Miracle?

We will now use an historical approach to consider something that is rarely discussed in analyses of serial murder — their absence. In short, why were there no serial killers active in Britain from the time that George Smith murdered his third victim, Margaret Lofty, on 18 December 1914, a month or so after the first Battle of Ypres, until Reginald Christie killed Ruth Fuerst in August 1943. This absence is even more noteworthy when compared with the number of serial killers who were active in Germany in the same period: between 1920 and 1940 there were a dozen documented cases of German serial killers, including the so-called "Vampire of Düsseldorf", Peter Kurten, who was charged with nine murders in April 1931; Fritz Haarmann, who killed 24 male prostitutes in Hanover between 1919 and 1924; and Bruno Ludke, who may have murdered as many as 51 people over a 15-year period that began in 1928.

How then are we to explain the absence of serial murderers in Britain while the Weimar Republic (1919–33) and the Third Reich (1933–45) had so many? What was it about our culture at that time that deterred serial murderers, while the Germans encountered them on such a regular basis?

The first possible explanation to consider is the lack of murder as a whole in Britain between the two world wars. This phenomenon was even noted at the time, with *The Times* suggesting that murder was so fully under control that only "one ... baffled the police in 1937"". British inter-war crime figures generally and the murder rate in particular have been investigated repeatedly ever since. Some historians and criminologists describe what happened as the "English miracle", given that the country's rising population was not matched by an increasing crime rate. In 1935, for example, according to *Criminal Statistics*, the annual compendium of recorded crime produced by the Home Office, in 1935 there were

> "Known to the police 87 cases of murder of 101 persons aged one year or over. In 41 cases, involving 50 victims, the murderer committed suicide; in 44 cases, involving 49 victims, two of whom had died following an illegal operation, 47 persons were arrested. In 2 cases involving 2 victims, 1 of whom had died following an illegal operation, no arrest was made."

These statistics give an appearance of certainty, finality and order. However, what are we to make of the fact that so many murder suspects (more than half in 1935) committed suicide or were found to be insane? What conclusions should we draw from longer-term trends that seem to indicate a century of stability? On average, there were only 50 murder trials in England and Wales each year between 1914 and 1939, and in only five of the 104 years between 1862 to 1966 were there fewer than 120 murders or more than 179. For example, between 1900 and 1924 there were on average 149.40 murders each year, and between 1925 and 1949 that average was almost identical at 148.76. But is that pattern a "remarkable miracle" or merely the result of statistical sleight of hand?

The historian Howard Taylor (1998) has been at the forefront of trying to interpret these crime figures and has come to a startling conclusion: they have been doctored; or, as he more carefully puts it, they are a "public illusion". In particular, "suicide" increased dramatically throughout the period that the murder rate remained stable. For example, in 1856, 1,314 suicides were recorded; by 1939, this figure had risen to a staggering 5,054. Looking more closely at the statistics for the later year gives us an insight into the "public illusion" that Taylor describes. According to various coroners' inquiries, there were 618 suicides but no homicides using poison; 706 suicides but only 29 homicides by hanging or strangulation; 247 suicides and 90 fatal accidents but only 21 homicides involving firearms; 787 suicides and 813 accidents but no homicides by drowning; and, finally, 422 suicides and 15 accidents but only 22 homicides involving cutting or piercing instruments. The implication is clearly that murders were often recorded as "suicides", which leads Taylor to conclude that "it was an open secret that most murders and suspicious deaths were not investigated".

So does any of this indicate that the absence of serial killers between the wars was merely the result of a failure of the police to record murder accurately? This is of course a possibility, but nonetheless very unlikely. Even if the police had not catalogued every murder, the press would undoubtedly have filled in the gaps with respect to a serial killer. After all, murder has always aroused great public interest, and a voracious print media has been well aware since the time of Jack the Ripper that stories of serial killing especially boost their circulation. In the 1930s, as at every other time in modern British history, the newspapers were filled with stories of murder, and as usual these proved irresistible to huge audiences.

While Taylor is probably right that many "suicides" of the interwar period were actually murders, with the press and public so keen to write and read about murder, it is fairly safe to assume that any serial killer active at the time would not have escaped detection for long. So, if the absence of serial killers in the inter-war period is not simply a statistical fiction, how else are we to account for it?

"There are people who say corpses don't talk, but indeed they do"

While there were a few famous forensic scientists in the Victorian and Edwardian periods, such as Sir Bernard Spilsbury, the growth in forensic science as a discipline occurred during the 1930s when the Home Office began to issue Forensic Science Circulars to local police forces, and various contemporary departmental committees emphasised the importance of science as a tool in criminal detection. Consequently, the Metropolitan Police established the first specialist, large-scale laboratory in 1935, and under Home Office guidance others were opened in Nottingham in 1936 and Birmingham and Cardiff in 1938. So, did a growing awareness of the role that forensic science might play in combating crime, and the increasing professionalisation of the discipline, contribute to the absence of serial killers during the inter-war years?

Key Term — Forensic Science

'Forensic' can be defined as that which is used in a court of law and therefore forensic science is simply the application of scientific — usually medical — knowledge to legal problems.

Two interesting autobiographies can help us to answer this question. The first is *Forty Years of Murder* by Professor Keith Simpson, first published in 1978 as his career was drawing to a close. The second was written by Simpson's secretary, Molly Lefebure: *Evidence for the Crown: Experiences of a Pathologist's Secretary* (1955). "Miss Molly", as she was known by those who worked with her, notes that "there are people who say corpses don't talk, but indeed they do ... and my goodness, how they talk! Everything about them talks. The way they look, the way they died, where they died, how they died." These two books offer a unique insight into how forensic science developed between the wars, and the role that the forensic scientist played in bringing murderers to justice.

Simpson enrolled at Guy's Hospital, London in 1924 and attended his first murder case at the end of 1934 at the York Hotel, opposite Waterloo Station. A parliamentary act of 1926 had given coroners the power to call upon any qualified medical practitioner to perform an autopsy, so many doctors with no pathology training, none of the appropriate equipment and ill-equipped laboratories were asked to conduct post-mortems. Simpson suggests that only a "handful" of people really knew what they were doing and had the necessary training and good instincts with respect to the issues of "obscure death or insurance, pensions, industrial, suicidal and homicidal cases". This handful, of course, included Simpson and his fame grew quite rapidly.

Simpson also reveals how the Home Office handled criminal evidence that needed to be scientifically evaluated before the opening of their specialist facility in 1935:

> "At the time all scientific work was handled by independent experts like Churchill, the firearm dealer, who was a shrewd businessman, jealous of the only competitor in his field, Major Burrard; Roche Lynch, a fine chemist at St Mary's Hospital, persuaded disastrously to undertake glass, hair, fibres, dust and blood-grouping work of which he had no experience whatever; Mitchell, an ink and handwriting expert (the latter has always been mistrusted); and dear old John Ryffel, 'Junior Home Office Analyst' (at sixty), my own teacher at Guy's. It was a quaint and unsatisfactory 'team' to cover laboratory service for the Home Office in crime investigation in England, but it committed no major blunders for nearly twenty years."

We have only Simpson's word that this motley team did not commit any major mistakes, and we have to wonder whether loyalty to colleagues and indeed his old teacher clouded his final assessment. Perhaps a more accurate impression can be gained from the fact that "blood-grouping work"—one of the staples of contemporary forensic science—was undertaken by someone who had been "persuaded disastrously" to carry out the task, and that he had no experience at all in this most sensitive area. Of course, Simpson may have exaggerated the level of incompetence to create an impression of "progress" in forensic science (largely as a result of his efforts) as the century wore on, but his naming of the individuals involved adds a degree of authenticity that is difficult to deny.

In 1941 Simpson employed Molly Lefebure. Molly had trained as a journalist before becoming Simpson's secretary, and her autobiography is a marvellous mine of information, providing a richness of detail that the scientifically minded Simpson probably thought irrelevant or perhaps inappropriate. She also sometimes contradicts his memory of events, and in general her account is the more convincing. For example, she says that she worked with Simpson before "the now famous Department of Forensic Medicine at Guy's" was established. At that time they were billeted in the curator's office in the Gordon Museum at the hospital, where

> "We did all our filing, report writing, correspondence and so forth, amidst a gleaming array of specimen jars in which floated grotesque babies, slashed wrists, ruptured hearts, stomach ulcers, lung cancers, bowel tumours, cerebral aneurisms and the like. Here too we generally took afternoon tea."

This is all very different from the description of clinical and efficient working conditions given by Simpson himself when he published his own book two decades later.

Molly also reveals how some of the specimens ended up in the jars in the curator's office. One day she encountered Simpson in a mortuary conducting a post-mortem on a young window cleaner who had slashed his throat and wrists after being abandoned by his lover. As Molly puts it, "the wrist wounds were especially fine ones", so Simpson wanted to remove one of them and preserve it for future reference. The only problem was how to transport it back to Guy's, until Simpson hit upon a solution. On her way to work, Molly had bought a pair of gloves: "So the new gloves went in my pocket, and I tripped out of the mortuary bearing the hand in the pretty little candy-striped paper carrier-bag which a chic shop-assistant had given me barely an hour ago."

Simpson claimed that he came across only a handful of criminal cases each year. But we should note that neither Simpson nor Lefebure mention every high-profile murder that was committed during the time they worked together. For example, neither describes the case of the "Blackout Ripper"—the pseudonym given to Gordon Cummins—a spree, rather than serial, killer who murdered four women in five days in 1942. However, it is fair to assume that between the wars there was a growing official awareness that science could aid criminal detection. As a consequence, relationships between the forensic scientists and the police developed rapidly in the 1930s, often prompted by the Home Office. Even so, based on what Simpson and Lefebure have written, it is hard to conclude that the development of forensic science contributed to the absence of serial killers in Britain during the inter-war years. So, perhaps it was the police who kept serial killers at bay?

Police Forces

During the inter-war period there were three different types of police force in England and Wales, and three different chains of command. First, there was the Metropolitan Police, who were responsible to the Home Secretary; second, the borough forces, such as Liverpool, Manchester and Birmingham, who were responsible to watch committees appointed by local councillors; and finally, the county forces, initially responsible to the police committees of the County Bench, and after 1889 to the standing joint committees of magistrates and county councillors.

As a result, throughout the inter-war years, there were regular attempts to centralise control of the police within the Home Office and weaken local authority control and influence. The Desborough Committee of 1919, for example, recommended a series of measures intended to bring greater uniformity to the police in the interests of "good order and efficiency": the establishment of uniform rates of pay; the creation of the Police Federation; the introduction of "F Division" within the Home Office to oversee, plan and direct the work of the police; and a rationalisation of the borough forces through a series of amalgamations of those boroughs with populations of less than 50,000. However, the committee's recommendations were never accepted, and subsequent attempts to abolish the borough forces—such as those made under the auspices of the Royal Commission on Local Government in the 1920s and the Select Committee of 1932—always failed. As late as 1939 there were still over 180 different police force areas.

These police boundaries are an important issue to consider especially as car ownership had become much more common. As early as 1921, almost a quarter of a million people owned cars, and the following year the launch of the Austin Seven—which cost £195 to buy and a penny a mile to run—brought the possibility of owning a small family car within reach for the masses. Just before the outbreak of war, the British automobile industry was producing close to 350,000 new cars each year. This growth in car ownership made offenders far more mobile than they had ever been before and, while the police might take note of police force boundary areas, criminals certainly did not.

Other new technologies—such as the telephone, telegraph and radio—could have been used by the police to alert neighbouring forces about suspicious characters who may have been heading their way. However, although telephones had been installed in almost every police station in the country by the mid-1930s, the forces were slow to utilise telegraph and radio communication, partly because of the expense of investing in these technologies but also because of the various forces' contrasting organizational cultures and conservatism.

If there were issues related to a lack of cooperation across police boundaries, there was a similar problem within forces. Specifically, nowadays it is considered crucial that detectives have good working relations with their uniformed colleagues. However, the Royal Commission of 1929 suggested that CID at Scotland Yard regarded itself as "a thing above and apart, to which the restrictions and limitations placed upon the ordinary police do not, or should not, apply". Similarly, the Departmental Committee on Detective Work, which reported in 1938, emphasised that detectives should have specialist training, which must have created a barrier between them and their uniformed colleagues. Detectives were also rather thin on the ground: just before the outbreak of war, the 58 county forces had only 581 detectives between them, while the 121 city and borough forces (excluding the Metropolitan and City of London Police) had only 1,198. In light of all this, it seems highly unlikely that improved detection prevented serial killing at this time.

So, if we can discount the contributions of the police generally as well as specialist detectives and forensic science between 1914 and 1943, how else are we to account for the absence of serial killers in this period?

Not Just Waiting for War

The 1920s and 1930s are usually summed up in a few images and events: the abdication of King Edward VIII in 1936; huge crowds attending the first Wembley Cup Final; and the General Strike that brought the country to a standstill. The historian and former Labour MP Roy Hattersley (2007) chooses another image "to represent the hard reality of Britain between the wars"—the "Jarrow Crusade". This choice reflects Hattersley's own interests and preoccupations, and his frequent use of the phrases "inter-war" and "between the wars"—not to mention the title of his book, *Borrowed Time*—reminds us that historians have tended to view this period as simply the prelude to war. Our knowledge that war with Germany would come in 1939 has led many authors to confine themselves to debating how prepared Britain was for battle, or to what extent the policy of appeasement made the coming conflict inevitable.

Another preoccupation of historians has been the mass unemployment that ravaged all the industrialised nations in the period. As the traditional industries of coalmining, steel and shipbuilding declined, many people were forced out of work: for instance, the number of coalminers declined from 1,083,000 in 1920 to 675,000 in 1938, and by the mid-1920s nine out of ten miners in Northumberland, Durham and South Wales had been laid off.

However, characterising the inter-war years in these ways ignores the fact that the majority of those who lived through it became better paid, were better dressed, lived in better houses, increasingly drove motor cars, took paid holidays, watched and attended sports events, went to the cinema, listened to the BBC and generally enjoyed higher standards of living. It also ignores the growth of the professional middle-class, and the development of new industries that kept the vast majority of people in work. More than this, in the 1920s and 1930s, those who were in paid employment—whether as professionals, tradesmen or labourers—became culturally more homogeneous, and the aspirations of one group were largely similar, or at least sympathetic, to those of another.

Even if we take Hattersley's Jarrow Crusade, we should remember that it was led by the Mayor and Lady Mayoress of Jarrow, who marched at the head of the column for the first 12 miles. Along the way the marchers were provided with food, shelter and clothing not only by local trade unions but by churches and ordinary members of the public. A service of support for the marchers was held in Ripon Cathedral, and Ellen Wilkinson—Member of Parliament for the borough—marched between 12 and 19 miles a day with her constituents. The march therefore seemed to demonstrate that people—*all* people—mattered: with universal suffrage having been achieved over the previous two decades, the life of every Briton was now inextricably bound up with that of every other Briton, irrespective of continuing disparities in wealth and status. Class divisions obviously existed, but these did not come close to producing either a fascist or a communist state in Britain at a time when such regimes were being established elsewhere. When war did break out, it was fought by a united people.

People Matter

Three factors support our suggestion that people mattered in Britain in the inter-war years. First, the development of universal suffrage; second, the various initiatives that were aimed at improving the lives of working-class people in terms of health, housing, and benefits made available to them in times of crisis; and, finally, the notion that the state had a responsibility to care for the elderly and educate the young.

As the First World War ended, the Representation of the People Act of 1918 trebled the electorate in the United Kingdom by giving the vote to every man over the age of twenty-one, and to women over thirty who owned property. Over 21 million people were now eligible to vote in the United Kingdom; 40 per cent of them — 8.5 million — were women. This extension of the vote to women has often been viewed as a "reward" for the role they played during the war, for example by working in munitions factories, on farms and even down coal mines or by driving buses. However, a variety of other reasons also contributed to the government's decision, not least the knowledge that it would appease moderate "suffragists" who might otherwise have supported the type of direct action employed by the "suffragettes" before the war.

The 1918 Act had some serious limitations. For example, it still denied the vote to older women who lived in rented property, as well as to many women in their twenties. True equality for women did not come until the Representation of the People Act of 1928 which extended the vote to all women over the age of 21 and, as a result, an extra five million names were added to the electoral register. This "flapper vote", as it is sometimes called, is often seen as crucial in bringing the Labour government of Ramsay MacDonald to power, although there is little evidence to support such an assertion. Nevertheless, by 1928 women were being viewed politically, legally and socially in a very different way to how they had been perceived in the Edwardian period, a time when they had been subsumed by the legal personalities of their husbands.

Between 1919 and 1922 Lloyd George's coalition government built over 200,000 "homes fit for heroes". Meanwhile, the Addison Housing Act of 1919 also stimulated house-building by offering subsidies to local authorities to launch construction projects aimed at providing accommodation for working-class families. In 1914 only about one per cent of the population rented council homes; by the outbreak of the Second World War that figure had increased to 14 per cent. In total about 4.3 million new homes were built between the wars, and by 1939 almost one family in three was living in a modern house that had been built after 1918. The Addison Housing Act was repealed in 1921, but the principle of offering subsidies to local authorities to build affordable homes for the working classes was maintained in the Chamberlain Housing Act of 1923, the Wheatley Housing Act of 1924 and in further Acts passed in 1930, 1933 and 1935.

It should be stressed that many people still lived in accommodation that was inadequate, that slum clearances were a major preoccupation of various governments during the inter-war years, and that house construction still struggled to keep up with demand. However, perhaps for the first time in British history, the government seemed genuinely concerned about the living conditions of the whole population, and that concern resulted in council houses that were brighter and airier, and had more bedrooms and better sanitary facilities than anything built before 1918. For example, by 1939 some 75 per cent of homes were wired for electricity. In turn, those who lived in these houses naturally wanted to take good care of them, and they started to spend more time inside rather than outside. Sales of vacuum cleaners rose from just over 200,000 in 1930 to 400,000 in 1938, while the sale of electrical cookers trebled during the same period. Other changes in society are indicated by the facts that, on the outbreak of war, just under 20 million newspapers were being sold each day, and 34 million people had access to a radio. Over eight million radio licence holders tuned in to the BBC, which had begun broadcasting in November 1922.

Better housing conditions certainly contributed to the improved health of the nation. A Ministry of Health had been established for the first time in 1919, and several Public Health Acts were passed in the 1930s. National Health insurance was introduced in 1911, and while it had its weaknesses, by 1936 19 million wage earners were covered by its provisions. They received a small cash payout when they were sick and could not work, enabling them to consult a doctor and receive treatment without charge. There were also more hospitals, more hospital beds, more nurses and more doctors: in 1911 there were 6.2 doctors per 10,000 of the population; by 1941 that had increased to 7.5 per 10,000. The Holidays and Pay Act of 1938 increased the number of people who were entitled to a paid week's holiday from one million in 1920 to eleven million in 1939. No doubt a significant proportion of them spent their week at one of the two hundred holiday camps that now dotted the British coastline. Others might simply have stayed at home, with occasional outings to the pictures for a treat: by the outbreak of war there were over four thousand cinemas, with the average weekly attendance over 20 million.

The Old Age Pension Amending Act was introduced in 1919, and was followed six years later by the Widows', Orphans' and Old Age Contributory Pensions Act, which organized pensions on a contributory basis and, as a result, made them available to many more people. The contributory principle distributed the cost of the pension between the worker, the employer and the state. By 1932, old age pensions of ten shillings a week were being provided to a total of 2,231,016 people aged 65 and over, with benefit provisions becoming more liberal and qualifying conditions—such as nationality and residency—becoming less stringent. As a result, state expenditure on pensions for those aged between 65 and 70 increased from £2,703,000 in 1928 to £16,381,000 in 1934.

Young people—and especially their education—became another preoccupation of successive governments. Between 1923 and 1933 a consultative committee chaired by Sir William Henry Hadow produced six reports about the education of young people from nursery school age onwards, making recommendations about the school leaving age, the provision of books in elementary schools and differentiation of the curriculum for boys and girls. Cumulatively, these reports totalled 1,500 pages. Hadow's 1926 report—*The Education of the Adolescent*—recommended a "regrading of education" so that there would be "primary" and "secondary" schools that would be based on "a fresh classification of the successive stages of education before and after the age of 11 plus", and proposed that the school leaving age should be raised to 15 by 1932, although this would not be achieved until the 1944 Education Act.

Of particular significance, Hadow's 1931 report, *The Primary School*, argued for separate infant schools and suggested that a primary school's curriculum should be "thought of in terms of activity and experience, rather than of knowledge to be acquired and facts to be stored". It also demanded a maximum class size of 40, special help for those children who were especially gifted or "retarded", and a training scheme so that teachers might meet the demands of the new primary school system. This system would be described today as "child centred", so there would be no standard curriculum but rather a focus on project work, which would allow the pupils to solve problems and make discoveries for themselves. In other words, children were to be valued and encouraged because, like everyone else in the 1930s, they mattered.

All of this should not obscure the fact that in the inter-war years many Britons endured considerable hardship and suffering, and significant disparities of wealth continued to exist. The key, though, is to understand that while the working class might no longer have been needed in the shipyards, down the pits or in the steelworks, their labour remained vital. They were simply required in different industries and different locations. Car production, for example, was increasingly concentrated in the South-East of England, so people relocated there from the coalfields of Wales and Yorkshire and the shipyards of the North-East. This undoubtedly created temporary difficulties, but for those who wanted to find employment, work was still available, and with it a stake in society and the possibility of improving both one's own life and that of one's family.

This is crucial when attempting to explain the absence of serial killers in Britain at a time when there were so many in Germany. The sheer scale of state initiatives and the willingness of successive governments to intervene in order to improve British citizens' lives indicate that people mattered in a way that they did not in the Weimar Republic and especially once Hitler had come to power. Under the Third Reich, Jews, gay people, gypsies, the elderly and the mentally-ill were all seen as irrelevant to the state's future and a drain on resources. The authorities' "solution" to this was extermination, which could be achieved actively, in the concentration camps, or passively, simply by failing to provide these people with any form of state protection.

Compare all of this with what was happening in Britain, where an inclusive society was being created, with every citizen viewed as vital to the future development of the nation, and the ties that bound people together becoming all-encompassing. Sport, literature, cinema and the media all helped to create a sense of what it meant to be British, part of which was the notion that one's fellow citizens were important. The government took the lead in fostering this concept by extending state protection to those groups that had previously been forced to manage for themselves as best they could. As they were increasingly viewed as having something to offer, they became more valued and therefore less vulnerable.

This lesson from our history, written from within the structural tradition of thinking about the phenomenon of serial murder, is that if people look out for one another and if their lives are valued and protected by the state, then it is much harder for a potential serial killer to achieve his objectives. How should we use this lesson to think about serial killing since the end of the Second World War? Do the lives of the elderly, babies and infants, young people leaving home, women who sell sexual services and gay men matter as much to us as they should? If they don't, might this be a vulnerability which serial killers exploit and which would, in turn, explain why there are so many more serial killers and victims of serial murder as our sample moves closer to the present day?

Revision

- On what basis should we exclude the following murderers from our list of British serial killers: Paul Brumfitt; Derrick Bird; Michael Lupo; Bible John?
- What period of British history saw the greatest number of serial murders?
- How are we to account for the absence of serial killers in the inter-war years?

Further Reading

A number of books were cited within the chapter. Specifically, we used Keith Simpson (1978), *Forty Years of Murder* (London: Grafton Books); Molly Lefebure (1955), *Evidence for the Crown: Experiences of a Pathologist's Secretary* (London: Heinemann); and Roy Hattersley (2007), *Borrowed Time: The Story of Britain Between the Wars* (London: Little, Brown). We also cited Howard Taylor's article (1988), "Rationing Crime: The Political Economy of Criminal Statistics since the 1850s", *Economic History Review*, Volume 51, No. 3, pp.569–90. You might also like to consult Phillip Jenkins (1988), "Serial Murder in England, 1940–1985", *Journal of Criminal Justice*, Volume 16, pp.1–15 which compares serial murder in Britain with the same phenomenon on Germany. There are a wide range of books about the police. A good place to start is Clive Elmsley (1991), *The English Police: A Political and Social History* (London: Longman).

SERIAL MURDER AND OCCUPATIONAL CHOICE

5

> "Serial killers, like society in general, have become geographically more mobile. Unlike their counterparts in earlier years, some serial murderers now travel around the country, leaving a trail of human carnage,"
>
> Jack Levin and James Alan Fox, 1985.

This chapter is concerned with the occupational choice(s) of British serial killers, and the potential significance of these choices within the phenomenon of serial killing. We are especially interested in those serial killers who chose occupations which had driving as a central feature of their work, even if Criminologists and Psychologists have been noticeably silent about the topic of driving and how this occupation might have a potential impact on how, where and when a serial killer might chose a victim and commit murder.

As we have discussed, one of the most difficult tasks in any study of serial killers remains defining what we mean when we label someone as a "serial killer" and, thereafter, in relation to this chapter how best to group them regarding their occupation(s). However, at the most basic level as far as labelling a serial killer is concerned there has to be a number of murders, and second there has to be a period of time between murders. All of this might seem simplistic, but confusions soon become evident. Egger (1984), for example, suggests a six point identification of the serial killer:

- there must be at least two victims;
- there is no relationship between perpetrator and victim;

- the murders are committed at different times and have no direct connection to previous or following murders;
- the murders occur at different locations;
- the murders are not committed for material gain;
- subsequent victims have characteristics in common with earlier victims (quoted in Creswell and Hollin, 1994: 3).

In a British context to assert that "there is no relationship between perpetrator and victim" would rule out such obvious serial killers as Dennis Nilsen and Frederick and Rosemary West. So too the idea that the murders must take place in different locations would also disqualify a killer who lures or forces his/her victims to a specific location to be killed from being labelled as a serial killer. This stipulation would again, for example, exclude the Wests, who killed at least nine young women at the same address in Gloucester.

So as to overcome some of these definitional and methodological difficulties, we have utilised in this chapter an established sample of British serial killers (Wilson, 2009), although we also bring this sample up-to-date. In particular we use it to identify what is known about the occupation of the serial killers that make up the sample and identify four distinct groups of occupations, which we have labelled: Drivers and Transient Dependent Work; Healthcare; Business; and, finally, Public and Personal Service.

However, before we begin to examine those serial murderers that held some form of legitimate employment, we also need to discuss those serial killers who had no formal employment or who were unemployed.

Unemployed Serial Killers

Twenty out of the 34 known British serial murderers identified were employed in the time period in which they committed their murders. With regards to those who were unemployed, no identifiable form of occupation could be determined. Out of the 14 serial murderers that lacked employment, nine turned to petty crime in an effort to receive some form of instrumental gain.

Key Terms — Instrumental and Expressive Crimes

Instrumental crimes are those offences in which the perpetrator seeks some form of monetary or material gain — likely objects that they cannot legitimately obtain. On the other hand, *expressive* crimes have no purpose except to achieve the act that is desired by the offender — this includes crimes such as murder and rape.

George Smith, otherwise referred to as the "Brides in the Bath" murderer, was convicted, and subsequently executed, for the murders of three women. Smith, whose criminal behaviour was apparent "by the age of nine" and had been sent to reform school for theft, would continue engaging in petty crime throughout the rest of his life. Smith's *modus operandi* would include moving from one town to the next, never more than "a few hundred miles" (Wilson, 2009: 68), and on meeting a suitable victim, would marry them, influence them into making a will in which their life savings would be left to him and shortly after murder them. Smith, who should obviously be considered not only to be a thief but also a bigamist, was clearly motivated by illegal financial gain.

Peter Manuel, known as the "Beast of Birkenshaw" was born in New York by Scottish parents before moving to Britain at the age of five (Wilson, 2009). Manuel, who was found guilty of murdering eight people, was not legitimately employed. Instead he earned a living through committing "property crimes" and, similar to George Smith, spent time "in and out of reform school" from an early age (p. 133).

Patrick Mackay, can be compared to George Smith and Peter Manuel and was, from a young age, attracting the attention of the school, mental health and criminal justice authorities. Mackay, while still in school, "got in trouble with the police for a series of increasingly serious offences" (p. 267) and by the time he had reached the age of 15 was described by a psychologist as a "'cold psychopathic kille'". Before and during Mackay's killing spree, he would target elderly women whenever he was in need of money and also killed an elderly priest.

Trevor Hardy, dubbed by the media as the "Beast in the Night", was convicted of murdering three teenage girls, and again shares similarities with those serial murderers already discussed within this category in that he too attracted the attention of the authorities from an early age:

> "His criminal career began when he was just eight years old. At the age of 15 years he was sent to the adult prison, HMP Strangeways, for burglary—the judge telling him that despite his young age he would be jailed 'for the public's protection'". (Wilson *et al,* 2010: 156)

It is evident that Hardy shares similarities with George Smith and Patrick Mackay, and that his lack of legitimate employment resulted in him turning to criminal acts, such as burglary, in order to receive financial rewards.

Michael Kitto "worked" alongside another British serial killer, Archibald Hall. and was subsequently found guilty for the murder of five people including an employer of Hall's. The motivation behind this serial killing "team" was that of financial reward, with the murders "executed in order to hide the crimes (mainly burglary and robbery)" (Grover and Soothill, 1997: 7). When the case of Archibald Hall and Michael Kitto is examined, Kitto is referred to as Hall's "criminal friend" and being "certainly unemployed at the time of the offences" (pp. 7–9).

Kenneth Erskine, referred to as the "Stockwell Strangler", was found guilty for the murder of seven elderly people. Erskine, who again shared similar traits to those serial murderers previously discussed within this category, had a troubled childhood and "by the age of 16 was already known by the police". In Erskine's case, one of the fundamental reasons for his eventual arrest was his need for money due to a lack of employment:

> "Erskine's first victim was 78-year-old Eileen Emms, a retired schoolteacher found dead in her Wandsworth home in early April.... Erskine had tucked her up so neatly in her bed that at first her family believed she had passed away quietly in her sleep.... it was only when she was about to be cremated they noticed her TV had been stolen and called the police." (Davey, 2009)

In the case of Erskine, his career in petty crime ultimately gave authorities a vital clue into the occupational background, or lack of, of the offender responsible for these particular murders.

Colin Ireland, known as the "Gay Slayer", was charged and subsequently found guilty for the murder of five gay men. Ireland was described as being motivated by the desire to "become known as a serial killer" (Ramsland, 2006: 50) as a consequence of having two broken marriages, no settled home, a childhood in borstal and a string of petty convictions for burglary or theft. After the murder of Peter Walker, a West End theatre director, Ireland phoned the *Sun* newspaper and said that his killing spree was a result of a "new year's resolution" (Ramsland, 2006: 50).

Mark Martin, the most contemporary example of a British serial murderer who was involved in crime as a means of financial reward, shares similarities with Colin Ireland. Like Ireland, Martin was motivated by the desire to become famous and "'relished" the thought of going down in history as his city's first serial killer". Martin, who was found guilty of murdering three women, was a homeless drifter whose *modus operandi,* which included the promise of giving his unknowing victims "cigarettes, clothes and a stolen credit card" (Wilson, 2009: 193), draws attention to the methods he implemented to obtain goods of financial worth whilst being homeless.

Of note is that, along with those serial murderers who lacked employment yet did not commit petty crime (see Peter Dinsdale; Steven Grieveson; Rosemary West; Stephen Griffiths), those serial killers who lacked employment were, on average, apprehended sooner than those who held some form of occupation. We will now shift focus towards those serial murderers that were employed at the time of their offending in an effort to shed some light as to how they were able to continually offend over a longer period of time in comparison to their unemployed counterparts.

Employed Serial Killers

With those British serial killers who lacked employment identified, attention will now move to those offenders who held some form of legitimate employment during the time in which they committed their known murders. Analysing the data presented in the following table, it was clear that there are four principal types of occupations that appear to be chosen by known British serial killers. These primary occupational roles are:

- driving and transitory dependent work;
- business;
- public and personal service; and, finally,
- healthcare.

These terms were generated and selected due to their generalised meaning in which a variety of occupations could be accommodated, but were also specific enough to separate two distinctly different occupations.

Occupations of British Serial Killers

Healthcare	Business	Public and personal service	Driving and transitory dependent work
Thomas Neill Cream Beverly Allitt Harold Shipman Colin Norris	John Haigh Ian Brady Myra Hindley Peter Moore	George Chapman Reginald Christie Archibald Hall Dennis Nilsen	Peter Sutcliffe John Duffy David Mulcahy Robert Black Fred West Levi Bellfield Peter Tobin Steve Wright

Healthcare

Thomas Neill Cream, Beverly Allitt, Harold Shipman and Colin Norris all murdered their victims under the guise of healthcare professionals. The earliest example is that of Thomas Neil Cream. Cream, otherwise referred to as the "Lambeth Poisoner", was noted to have been interested in becoming a doctor at an early age and "earned his degree of Doctor of Medicine and Master of Surgery in 1876". With regards to how his occupation affected his criminal behaviour, Cream would use his status as a doctor to influence his victims into taking harmful substances. More specifically, Cream would offer "capsules containing Strychnine" to his victims under the guise that it was a medication to improve their complexions. Cream is an example of a serial murderer that used his occupational status to influence his unknowing victims into taking a harmful substance without questioning his motivation.

It was not until the 1990s, almost a century after Cream, that the next known British serial murderer who worked within the healthcare profession was identified. Beverly Allitt, referred to as either the "Killer Nurse" or more commonly the "Angel of Death", targeted young children within the hospital in which she worked. Allitt, who has since been identified as having a serious personality disorder known as Munchausen Syndrome by Proxy, in which the individual is "characterised by physical or psychological symptoms that are feigned, exaggerated, or self-induced" (Ramsland, 2006: 46), was convicted of murdering four children. Allit had access to high dosages of morphine, which she injected into each of her victims (Ramsland, 2006: 47).

The next case to be discussed is the most prolific example of serial murder in Britain. Harold Shipman, who had been found guilty of the murder of 15 of his patients, but later linked to 215 over a 23-year period , was a well-loved GP with a number of close friends. Like all of the cases previously discussed within this particular category, Shipman's *modus operandi* consisted of the following factors:

> "Shipman's *modus operandi* was to identify vulnerable elderly patients and inject them with intravenous diamorphine, either on home visits or occasionally in the surgery. He often falsified their records, for instance making it appear that they had recently been complaining of chest pains" (Misselbrook, 2010: 85).

Taking the above statement into consideration, there are several similarities and themes emerging in regards to how British serial murderers used the advantages required through working within the "healthcare" profession to commit their offences, most notably the easy access to a wide array of potentially lethal substances. While Shipman shares these common similarities with other British serial murderers who worked within the medical profession, he also differs in some key areas that could perhaps help better understand why he was able to kill so many of his patients before raising suspicions. One of the most notable differences between Shipman and those serial murderers discussed previously within this category is his selection of victims—elderly patients. This is already in stark contrast to Beverly Allit, who murdered young children, and Thomas Neil Cream, who targeted young women. The types of victims targeted by these particular serial murderers would arguably attract more suspicion as opposed to the elderly patients of Shipman. A second important factor to consider is the variety of positions that are within the "healthcare" profession. With regard to Shipman, his position as a general practitioner within his community resulted in him being a much loved and well-respected family doctor for 25 years. Shipman's status within the healthcare profession also came with a high level of respect; respect that kept the fact that he was a serial murderer virtually secret from everyone's notice.

Colin Norris is the most contemporary example of a British serial murderer that worked within the "healthcare" profession[1]. Norris, titled the "Killer Nurse" and the "Angel of Death" by the media,

1. Here we should note that there is evidence that Norris may have been the victim of a miscarriage of justice, although he remains in custody whilst his case is considered by the Criminal Cases Review Commission.

worked as a staff nurse at Leeds General Infirmary and St James's Hospital in Leeds. Similar to the serial murderers previously discussed who worked within this profession, Norris would use lethal dosages of substances which, in his case, was insulin in order to murder his victims who happened to also be his patients. The case of Norris, who was found guilty in 2008 of murdering four of his patients, gives an insight into why the medical profession has been the occupational choice for four known British serial murderers. Detective Chief Superintendent Gregg, quoted in the *Telegraph*, highlights not only why Norris was able to kill four of his patients, but also what is arguably the most important factor as to why serial murderers choose this particular profession:

> "What has shone out through this investigation and trial is the absolute dedication of nursing and medical professionals. Colin Norris is an exception to that. While others around him were duly caring for their patients, he was looking for opportunities to kill them by poisoning them with insulin" (Stokes and Britten, 2008)

The above quote draws attention to the fact that working within the "healthcare" profession would give an individual intending to commit murder the opportunity required in order to do so. Through the discussion of the four identifiable British serial murderers within this category, it is evident that they were given access to both potential harmful substances, and patients who were depending upon them for medical assistance. Both of these factors contribute significantly in giving the offender opportunity to elicit their criminal behaviour without raising initial suspicions.

Business

John Haigh, often referred to as the "Acid Bath Murderer", spent a brief period of time in prison during the Second World War "in which he served 15 months for conspiracy to defraud and obtaining money by false pretences" (Wilson, 2009: 117). Taking into consideration Haigh's criminal history, it would seem reasonable to fit him into the category of "unemployed"—in which most of these serial murderers engaged in petty crime as a means of achieving financial reward. Despite this, though, there are important factors that have resulted in him being positioned under "Business". These factors include the knowledge that he was in employment for much of his adult life, working as an "insurance sales clerk", "a clerk in an advertising firm" and an accountant for an engineering company. Despite Haigh often being fired from his jobs for various reasons, and being involved in criminal activities such as fraud, he has been placed within "Business" due to the nature of the work in which he was involved in, and also because of Haigh's regular employment despite his offending behaviour.

Ian Brady and Myra Hindley, due to the nature in which they committed their crimes together, and the fact that they both had occupations that fit into the "Business" grouping, will be discussed jointly. Brady and Hindley, otherwise known as the "Moors Murderers", murdered five children between the period of 1963-1965. Brady and Hindley are one of the earliest examples of serial murderers operating under a *folie à deux*. Birch (1994) attempts to answer how such a unique phenomenon in an already rare criminal act that is serial murdering could come to existence:

> "For Myra Hindley, Ian Brady became the God that replaced her Catholicism. But why she was attracted to his 'theology' of fascism and nihilism, and why she became a participant in those brutal murders, are questions which have vexed her friends and commentators alike." (Birch, 1994: p. 42)

Taking the above statement into consideration, it would seem that Brady was the individual with the already established delusion, and out of the two, the one with the genuine psychotic disorder, otherwise known as the primary case. Hindley, on the other hand, was the individual who gradually developed similar symptoms and is considered the secondary case. This, of course, is purely a psychological perspective with, as Birch highlights, many people still searching for answers to questions continually being asked regarding serial murdering "teams". Brady shares many similarities with John Haigh in that he too was involved in petty crime prior to gaining employment. Similar to Haigh, Brady has been positioned within the occupational category of "Business" as, at the age of 21, he found employment as a stock clerk at Millwards, a chemical firm. Hindley began working at the age of 14 for various employers in offices (Birch, 1994), and eventually worked within the same business organization as Brady, more specifically as a "shorthand typist" (p. 38). Hindley, who evidently worked within a "Business" environment, has also been placed within the same occupational category as Brady. Similar to Fred and Rosemary West, in which only Fred West held occupations that required the use of a vehicle yet both offenders utilised a car when committing their crimes, Ian Brady and Myra Hindley also used vehicles whilst they offended despite the lack of transport required within their occupations.

It is important to acknowledge here the use of vehicles for Brady and Hindley, primarily due to the unique way in which they incorporated them in order to commit their offences. With the use of a car, Hindley would offer a lift to a potential victim, possibly aware that people would more than likely trust an unknown woman as opposed to a man that they did not know. An example of this is their first victim, 16-year-old Pauline Read, who accepted a lift from Hindley while she was walking to a dance at the Railway Worker's Social Club in Manchester (Wilson, 2009: 222). Berry-Dee and Morris (2008) note that, due to Brady only having a licence to ride a motorcycle, and knowing that they would need a car to abduct their victims, Hindley took lessons in order to learn how to drive (p. 119). In some instances, with access to both a car and a motorcycle, Brady would follow behind Hindley's car. During these occasions Brady would, once spotting a potential victim, signal with his headlamp to Hindley which stood for: "There is another one here, stop and talk to this individual" (p. 121). This method offered this serial murdering "team" an instrumental advantage that is unique to them, with all further mobile serial murderers using only one vehicle at any given time.

Peter Moore, often referred to as the "Man in Black", was a theatre manager situated in Wales. Whilst the fact that Moore, who in fact owned numerous theatres, would often drive back and forth between these establishments (Wilson, 2009: 116), his role as manager takes precedence. Another important factor to consider is that, unlike those serial murderers that were transient dependent and had no fixed occupational base, Moore had fixed work locations that would remain steady over time. It is important to still acknowledge that driving was a substantial component of his occupation. With regards to the relationship between his occupational lifestyle and his criminal offending, Moore had been fined for being in possession of a truncheon that was being concealed in his van that "he used to 'drive to and from his various cinemas'" (p.116).

Public and Personal Service

George Chapman, otherwise referred to as the "Borough Poisoner", offered services as a barber and lived within the Whitechapel area of London. Chapman's business, while successful for a time, ultimately closed and he changed trades and worked in a pub. Whilst Chapman may have owned his own business, both his occupations as a barber, and later a publican, both offered services to the general public.

The next serial murderer, Reginald Christie, offered his service to the general public in the form of volunteering as a wartime constable charged with keeping the peace during a time of war and had been, at one time, a soldier. In 1939 Christie became a special constable in the War Reserve Police. In the case of Christie, war offered him the opportunity to gain authority and consequently respect from those around him. This also helped to keep his criminal activities secret.

Archibald Hall, who, alongside petty criminal Michael Kitto, murdered five people. Hall had a rather extensive career as a personal butler to a number of wealthy individuals. Unfortunately, the very people he offered his services to would often become the target of his crimes. Interestingly, a car was used in order to transport his and Michael Kitto's victims, so that when the vehicle was searched the police found the body of Donald Hall in the boot.

Dennis Nilsen, often referred to as the "Kindly Killer", is another key example of a serial murderer that worked in various occupations that would be regarded as being "Public and Personal Service" in nature. Nilsen, similar to that of Donald Nielson, served time in the army. Nilsen spent eleven years within the army (Masters, 1995: 80) and, upon voluntary discharge due to becoming "more disenchanted with the military mind" and feeling "increasingly uncomfortable on the side of the 'oppressors'" (p.80), he changed occupation. Nilsen's next two occupational choices, the police service followed by a position as a civil servant (Wilson, 2009: 13), again fit neatly within this grouping. While it is debatable that Nilsen's occupation as a civil servant, in which he worked in a job centre (Masters, 1995: 4) would have resulted in a lessening of authority, it would seem he took his job seriously and in the same disciplined manner that he would have developed during his time in the army:

> "His intelligence and his powers of marshalling essential arguments were admired, as was his capacity for organization. His sense of equilibrium was secretly deplored; there appeared to be no allowance made in his mind for the virtues of compromise" (Masters, 1995: 4).

While Nilsen was, as the above statement highlights, criticised for his behaviour, his occupational choices would, similar to those serial murderers already discussed within this category, prove useful for him in regards to committing his crimes. For example, in regards to those people who knew him, any thoughts they may have had regarding Nilsen and his criminal behaviour could have been potentially averted due to his occupation and status within his work environment.

Driving and Transitory Dependent Work

This occupational category appears to be the most dominant, with approximately 40 per cent of those serial murderers recognised as holding valid forms of occupation falling into this set. This group came into prominence in the mid-1970s primarily due to the fact that vehicles had become much more accessible to the general public and that, due to the road networks expanding in order to meet the increase in car ownership, more and more locations became accessible that were before difficult to reach.

Peter Sutcliffe, dubbed the "Yorkshire Ripper" by the media, worked as a long distance lorry driver who went as far as to name one of his trucks "Willy", which of course is a shortening of the name William—Sutcliffe's middle name. Sutcliffe was convicted of killing 13 women and attacking seven others between 1975 and 1980 and, as the name given to him by the press implies, the bodies of his victims were often mutilated (Wilson, 2009: 77).

Robert Black, while already serving life imprisonment for three other murders, was charged and subsequently found guilty in October 2011 of killing nine-year old Jennifer Cardy 30 years earlier in Ballinderry, County Antrim, Northern Ireland. Black, who has been described as "every parent's worst nightmare", drove through Britain in search of potential victims, using his blue transit van as a means to capture and transport his victims (Wilson, 2009: 223).

John Duffy and David Mulcahy were serial rapists and murderers who terrorised railway stations throughout the South-East of England including the North and West areas of London (Canter, 2005: 173). At work both men appeared to be inseparable. "They worked at Westminster City Council, where Mulcahy was a plumber and Duffy a carpenter" and Mulcahy engaged in work outside of the council by moonlighting as a mini-cab driver. At the time when the attacks took place, the police and the media were unsure if the offences were being committed by one, or two assailants. This led to the media dubbing the attacks as the work of the "Railway Rapist" (p. 174). Forensic psychologist, David Canter, who worked alongside the police to help apprehend the attacker(s), notes that not only did the offenders literally travel over a wide geographical area in search of potential victims (p. 174), but that those involved were also going through a much more personal, psychological journey:

> "This case showed a person on a vicious journey, starting with unplanned, opportunistic rape and leading to planned, brutal murder. What if this mental journey was reflected in the killer's journeys to his crimes?" (Canter, 2005: 175)

The case of Duffy and Mulcahy offers an interesting perspective into mobile serial murderers in regards to how the instrumental and psychological factors of travelling are intertwined. Canter, in his work for the police, discovered that as time passed and more attacks were being reported, the locations of these horrific events seemed to change, spreading outwards like a "disease" (p. 175).

We now move onto one of the more media obsessed cases of serial murder, Fred and Rosemary West. It is important to note here that, while Rosemary West has been classified under "Unemployed", she played a fundamental part in Fred West's offences and as a result of this will be included in this analysis (For an opposing view see Masters, 1996). This serial murdering team are an example of the rare *folie à deux* among British serial murderers. Fred West, who worked as a mobile odd-job labourer and, at one point, an ice-cream seller operating in a van, was suspected of killing eleven women whilst Rosemary was convicted of killing ten. Their own daughter, Heather West, was among the list of confirmed victims. One of the more startling aspects of the West case is the sheer period of time that they were active, killing young women over a 20-year period during the years of 1967–1987. The Wests lived at 25 Cromwell Street, a residence that housed "horrific secrets" (Bennett, 1995), and has since been demolished. Fred and Rosemary West incorporated the use of a vehicle as part of their method of luring lone, young women from the roadside and into their car (Wilson, 2009: 201). This is not the only example of women being used to "lure" victims. Myra Hindley, one part of the "Moors Murderers", was also used to ensure their victims cooperation in regards to entering their vehicle.

Levi Bellfield, otherwise referred to as the "Bus Stop Killer", worked primarily as a wheel clamper during the period in which he murdered his three victims (Wansell, 2011: 147). Bellfield is an example of how the geographically transient serial murderer is finding it harder to evade detection from the authorities, as he was ultimately apprehended due to being caught on CCTV (p.194–195).

Peter Tobin, similar to Fred West, worked as a mobile odd job labourer. Tobin, who was charged and convicted for the murder of three women, was a handyman by occupation. Tobin again offers a completely different perspective on the "geographically transient" serial murderer. Tobin, armed with the skills necessary to be a handyman, is known to have used false names during particular jobs. This conscious decision to hide his true identity gives insight into the level of premeditation Tobin engaged in before committing his crimes. In some respects, Tobin has more in common with George Smith, than some of the more contemporary examples such as Peter Sutcliffe or Robert Black. This is primarily due to the nature in which Tobin travelled. Like Smith, Tobin, as a result of his occupation, would frequently move from house to house, often leaving a victim behind. This constant moving from one part of the country to another also ensures that the serial murderer crosses multiple police force boundaries. This important issue is often present with geographically transient serial murderers, and can often create "linkage blindness".

Key Term — Linkage Blindness

The term linkage blindness was coined in 1984 and highlights a fundamental issue with law enforcement with regards to serial murder investigations. Law enforcement officers occasionally fail to see or are thwarted from seeing outside their own jurisdictional obligations. This is primarily due to their responsibility usually ceasing at the boundary of their jurisdiction.

The most recent case of a "geographically transient" serial murderer is Steve Wright, otherwise known as the "Suffolk Strangler". There are evident similarities between Wright and Peter Sutcliffe. Both of these men worked in what would be considered menial and low-skilled jobs, with Wright at one stage being a forklift truck driver. Wright and Sutcliffe also targeted prostitutes, with the former convicted with the murders of five women during a six week campaign of murder. Where the two differ is that, while Sutcliffe consciously chose a profession which would put him in an environment he felt comfortable in, Wright was much more ambitious, entering low-skilled labour most likely due to financial predicaments:

> "He's embraced a culture that rewards hard work with upward mobility, and yet he can't find his place in that world ... he can't move upwards. He's denied power through his class, his lack of education and skills ... power that he feels is rightly his." (Wilson, 2009:54)

It is arguable that whatever fantasies Wright had regarding killing another human being, they were ultimately able to grow and develop during these periods of working in jobs that required little in the way of mental attention.

This chapter has sought to outline the occupations held by known British serial murderers. In doing so, we have suggested that there were four predominant occupational fields which British serial murderers fall under—along with those that lacked any form of legitimate employment. These occupational groupings are described earlier in this chapter. This analysis determined that the occupational grouping that involved a dependency on transport was the most commonly selected form of employment for British serial murderers, with a total of eight individual offenders compared to the other grouping's four.

In the next chapter we will attempt to explore why this is the case by presenting a case study of the serial killer Peter Sutcliffe. Were these serial killers drawn to these occupations because of their desire to be able to commit murder? Did working in this particular type of work environment—and perhaps the solitude that it provides—ignite some latent fantasy that was ultimately nurtured, developed and consequently acted upon? Finally, what role did the vehicle play when being driven by someone with intentions to commit murder?

Revision

- What is "linkage blindness"?
- What is the difference between instrumental and expressive crimes?
- How many British serial killers lacked employment?
- Does the average offending period of employed serial killers differ from those that lacked employment?
- What is the most commonly selected form of occupation for British serial killers?

Further Reading

Academic research into the significance of occupational choice is in its infancy and, as a result, the amount of readily available literature is sparse. Despite this lack of scholarly work, though, there are a number of texts that the reader may find useful. For example, J McClellan (2008), "Delivery Drivers and Long-Haul Truckers: Traveling Serial Murderers", *Journal of Applied Security Research* 3(2) 171–190; K Soothill and D Wilson (2005), "Theorising the Puzzle that is Harold Shipman", *Journal of Forensic Psychiatry and Psychology* 16(4) 685–698; and A Lynes, D Wilson and C Jackson (2012), "Zola and the Serial Killer: Robert Black and *La Bête Humaine*", *International Journal of Criminology and Sociology,* 1(1) 69–80. There are also a number of "true crime" books that provide an in-depth account of the occupational history of British serial killers, most notably G Wansell (2011), *The Bus Stop Killer*, London: Penguin Books; and M Bilton (2003), *Wicked Beyond Belief: The Hunt for the Yorkshire Ripper,* London: Harperpress. These last two sources are of particular note due to both providing an in-depth biography of serial killers who held transient oriented occupations.

A number of other references appear within the text. Chief amongst these is Katherine Ramsland (2006), *Inside the Minds of Healthcare Serial Killers: Why They Kill,* New York: Praeger and D Wilson, H Tolputt, N Howe and D Kemp (2010), "When Serial Killers Go Unseen: The Case of Trevor Joseph Hardy," *Crime Media Culture*, Vol 6 No 2, pps 153–167.

CASE STUDY: PETER SUTCLIFFE

6

"In this truck is a man
Whose latent genius if
Unleashed would rock the
Nation, whose dynamic energy
Would overpower those
Around him: better let
Him sleep?"

Note written by Peter William Sutcliffe aka The Yorkshire Ripper found in his truck

Chapter 5 provided an in-depth analysis into the occupational choices of British serial killers. Through this analysis, it was shown that the most commonly selected type of occupation tended to have driving as a key component of their work, with eight serial killers having held such employment at the time in which they committed their known offences. Of these eight serial killers, Peter Sutcliffe, often referred to as the "Yorkshire Ripper", is arguably the most infamous and, as a result, his life and crimes have been extensively documented. Given this extensive secondary literature, Sutcliffe presents as a suitable subject for a case study with regards to the significance of driving as an occupational choice for serial killers.

Key Term — Case Study

In the social sciences a case study is a research method which involves an in-depth and detailed investigation of a single person, group, activity or community (the "case"). The fact that the investigation is so detailed allows inferences to be drawn about more general phenomena.

Measuring the *significance* of driving as an occupational choice will be achieved by separating this case study into two distinct categories entitled the "instrumental" and the "psychological". The former relates to how Sutcliffe's occupation and, through extension, his vehicle, might have practically influenced or aided his offending behaviour. For example, did he gain situational awareness regarding suitable stalking locations whilst supposedly engaging in work related activities? How did driving allow him to enter and leave the scenes of his crimes? The latter refers to how Sutcliffe's occupation may have influenced his behaviour at a more subjective, or mental level, such as whether, for example, the long periods that he spent by himself, isolated behind the steering wheel, might have assisted in the development of his criminal fantasies.

Sutcliffe committed all of his crimes with the aid of transport and so fits the requirements necessary for our case study. Not only did he drive various vehicles in order to carry out his crimes, but he also consciously chose a profession that would result in him being surrounded by mechanics and discussion about cars and lorries. Through analysing the statements made by Sutcliffe to the West Yorkshire Police following his arrest and subsequent charging (see Bilton, 2003), the reasons as to why Sutcliffe decided to use a vehicle in order to carry out his crimes, both for practical and psychological reasons becomes much clearer. The over-arching aim of this case study is not to offer another reason, or interpretation, as to why serial killers commit the crimes that they do, but to gain a deeper level of understanding as to the role a transient oriented occupation and, by extension, a vehicle, can potentially play when being driven by someone determined to commit murder.

Case Overview

Lorry driver Peter Sutcliffe attacked and murdered women, predominantly sex workers, over a five-year period—attacking women in a number of locations but including Bradford, Leeds, and Manchester (Bilton, 2003). In this five-year period, in which the authorities considered hundreds of possible suspects (including, at one, time, Sutcliffe himself), Sutcliffe murdered 13 women and attacked and injured many others.

His first victim was Wilma McCann, who was murdered on 30 October 1975. Wilma, from the Chapeltown district of Leeds, was a mother of four and was known to offer sexual services for money. Sutcliffe, exhibiting a similar *modus operandi* that would be present in future murders, hit her twice with a hammer prior to stabbing her 15 times in the abdomen, chest, and neck (Bilton, 2003). Traces of semen were also found on her underwear, which suggested a sexual motive. Despite a widespread inquiry, which consisted of over 150 police officers and 11,000 interviews, no culprit was identified until five years later upon Sutcliffe's eventual arrest. Forty-two year-old Emily Jackson, who was found murdered in Leeds in 1976, was Sutcliffe's next victim. She too exchanged sexual services for money due to financial difficulties (Bilton, 2003)—she was found with 51 puncture wounds.

Nineteen-seventy-seven would prove to be one of the most infamous years in the 'Ripper' investigation, with Sutcliffe murdering four women—28-year-old Irene Richardson, 32-year-old Patricia Atkinson, 16-year-old Jayne MacDonald, and 20 year-old Jean Jordan. Of these victims, three were known sex workers, although Jayne had just left school and was working as a shop assistant. Jayne's death marked something of a turning point not only for the investigation but also, with the realisation that any woman could potentially be a victim, public perception and support for the identification and apprehension of the killer.

The following year Sutcliffe attacked and killed 21-year-old Yvonne Pearson, another sex worker, but whose remains were only found three months after being murdered due to Sutcliffe hiding her body under a discarded sofa. Sutcliffe would go on to murder two more women in 1978—18-year-old Helen Rytka and 40-year-old Vera Millward—both were sex workers and both were bludgeoned and stabbed to death (Bilton, 2003). It was almost a year before Sutcliffe claimed his next victim, 19-year-old Josephine Whitaker, a bank clerk whom Sutcliffe attacked whilst she was on her way home. His next murder, that of 20-year-old university student Barbara Leach, would mark Sutcliffe's third murder of a woman who did not sell sexual services and, as a result, public outcry in relation to the failures of the 'ripper' investigation reached fever pitch. Despite this public outcry it would take the authorities another year before finally apprehending Sutcliffe.

Nineteen-eighty-one was the year that Sutcliffe was identified as the 'ripper' but before his arrest he claimed the lives of two more women. Whilst waiting to be tried for drunk driving in 1980, Sutcliffe attacked and subsequently murdered 47-year-old Marguerite Walls and 20-year-old Jacqueline Hill. Both women came from respectable backgrounds, with Marguerite working as a civil servant and Jacqueline studying English at university (Bilton, 2003). Here we might note that this change in victim selection may have been a result of Sutcliffe's growing confidence at the thought of not getting caught. Indeed Sutcliffe may have continued to kill other women if it hadn't had been for a routine police stop on a winter's night.

On 2 January 1981, the police stopped Sutcliffe, who was with 24-year-old sex worker Olivia Reivers. The police discovered that Sutcliffe's car was fitted with false number plates and, as a result, he was arrested. The next day police returned to the scene of the arrest and discovered a knife, hammer and some rope that he had discarded when he had temporarily left their presence telling them he needed the toilet. Sutcliffe was questioned for two days before finally admitting that he was the "Yorkshire Ripper".

At his trial, Sutcliffe pleaded guilty to manslaughter on the grounds of diminished responsibility. He claimed that he was following orders given to him by God to rid the world of sex workers. Despite this defence, Sutcliffe was found guilty of murder on all counts and was subsequently sent to HMP Parkhurst to serve his sentence. Whilst he was found sane at his trial, in 1984 Sutcliffe was diagnosed as having paranoid schizophrenia and was thereafter sent to Broadmoor Hospital, where he remains to this day. An appeal initiated on his behalf for a release date was rejected in 2010 so that Sutcliffe—who has since started to use his mother's maiden name of "Coonan"—will never be released back into the community.

Occupational History

Sutcliffe had an extensive history of working in either labour intensive or transient orientated occupations that tended to be solitary and were more technical in nature. He was described as being shy as a child and also withdrawn and passive (Wilson, 2009), and appeared to carry on these characteristics of being isolated and removed from others as an adult. After leaving school, his first known employment involved a short period working as a gravedigger, which consisted of mainly menial labour-oriented tasks and duties (Bilton, 2003). It was at this time Sutcliffe appeared to demonstrate a rather dark and macabre sense of humour, and seemingly relishing the solitary nature of the job. Interestingly, it was during Sutcliffe's time working as a gravedigger that he said God first spoke to him and subsequently ordered him to murder sex workers (Bilton, 2003).

Sutcliffe thereafter moved from his grave digging profession towards more factory-oriented employment at Baird Television Ltd, where he worked on a packaging line. Again, Sutcliffe appeared to be drawn to work environments that oriented on physical and labour intensive activities. This trend towards working in such labour intensive occupations continued, with Sutcliffe leaving Baird when he was asked to become a traveling salesman and subsequently began to work nightshifts as a factory worker for Anderton International. In 1975 Sutcliffe was made redundant and he used the redundancy money to acquire a heavy goods vehicle licence. Sutcliffe passed the HGV test Class 1 at Steeton driving school on June 4th—two days after his 29th birthday. On obtaining his HGV license, he became employed for a company as a lorry driver in September 1975. This work, which consisted of short-distance and medium-distance hauls all over the North and the Midlands of the UK, would play an instrumental part in Sutcliffe's increasing awareness of Britain's road networks:

> ...He used the experience to familiarise himself with the network of motorways and trunk-roads linking his destinations to each other and to West Yorkshire. He also became an authority on the best access routes to many town and city centres, to some of which he was already less than a stranger (Burn, 2011: 135).

Sutcliffe, after leaving this particular job, continued to make use of his HGV licence and took up employment as a lorry driver for T & W H Clark (Holdings) Ltd, which was situated on the Canal Road Industrial Estate in Bradford. It would be while employed by this company and in this job that Sutcliffe would commit the majority of his known offences. In examining Sutcliffe's employment history, it is apparent that he appeared to be drawn to those that consisted of either labour intensive worik or that were transient oriented. How might his employment history relate to his offending history?

Offending History

Sutcliffe's first recorded offence involving a sex worker would set the template for his future murders. For Sutcliffe, who was known as a regular visitor to the red light district of Bradford, often in the early days with his friend Trevor Birdsall, appeared to commit his first known offence after an altercation with a sex worker in 1969—six years prior to committing his first murder. Indeed Sutcliffe was in fact arrested in Bradford's red light district in 1969 for having a hammer in his possession and which the police believed he had intended to use to commit burglary. In fact Sutcliffe, whilst in the company of his friend Birdsall, assaulted and attacked a sex worker with a rock that he had placed within a sock. In this particular instance, Sutcliffe, supposedly angered by the attitude of the sex worker, left Birdsall alone in his car and, upon his return, informed Birdsall that he had tried to attack the sex worker (Wilson, 2009). Sutcliffe also displayed signs of sexual deviancy whilst employed as a gravedigger, in which many of his co-workers were concerned about his constant comments and thoughts towards necrophilia when around dead bodies. Sutcliffe's history of violence towards women, in particular the case in 1969 when in the company of Birdsall, clearly set a template for his future offences, which were heavily influenced by the environmental conditions, or cues that his occupation positioned him within close proximity.

Key Term — Crime Template

A concept deriving from Crime Pattern Theory, a perspective housed within Environmental Criminology, crime templates are formed through past experiences and actions and subsequently influence future offending behaviour and decisions. Specifically, as Brantingham and Brantingham (1993) argue, "past actions and activities help 'drive' current actions just as a car might 'drive itself' to work or to the supermarket." (p. 269)

Peter Sutcliffe — A Case Study of Serial Murder

Sutcliffe made a number of statements to the police which are reproduced in Bilton (2003), *Wicked Beyond Belief: The Hunt for the Yorkshire Ripper.* Through an analysis of these official statements to the police several themes emerge, which can be viewed as being both instrumental and psychological, although we should also remember that these statements sought to establish Sutcliffe's guilt and therefore have to be used with care. In other words, these statements have a specific purpose within the police investigation and were being used to establish whether a charge could be brought against Sutcliffe. This formal purpose has to be remembered when we reconsider these statements for our own analysis.

The most apparent instrumental advantage that Sutcliffe discusses is the ability to flee the scene of the crime. This capability to "geta-way" offers an immediate important benefit for the culprit. In being able to quickly leave the crime scene, the offender has time to return home, or to a place they consider "safe". There they might remove any trace of physical evidence that could place them at the scene of the crime. While Sutcliffe does not explicitly state that he would return home in order to dispose of any potential evidence, he would occasionally make comments such as "I found that I didn't have any blood on my clothes" and "I looked at my clothes at the garage I saw that I had blood on the bottom of my jeans… I took my jeans off and rinsed them under the cold tap" (Bilton, 2003: 695–698). Subtle remarks such as these convey the importance of being able to leave the scene of the crime, and by doing so offering to the offender an opportunity to compose themselves, carefully assess the conditions of their clothes and appearance, and thus being able to conceal any apparent signs that they might be responsible for the recently committed crime.

In his formal statements Sutcliffe acknowledges that he would travel to a number of different locations in his search for potential victims, thus enabling him to access areas that would otherwise be inaccessible without the use of a vehicle. This ability to see the "bigger picture" while committing serial murder provides the perpetrator with a number of advantages. Sutcliffe touches upon the primary benefit of being able to travel across a wide geographical area. For example, he states that 'I realised things were hotting up a bit in Leeds and Bradford. I decided to go to Manchester to kill a prostitute' (Bilton, 2003: 703). With access to a vehicle, Sutcliffe was consequently able to continue feeding his desires to kill women without the fear of raising suspicion in one particular area. Sutcliffe not only visited Manchester, but also 'the red light districts in Leeds, Bradford, Halifax, and York' (p. 742). This seemingly sporadic selection of locations not only keeps the police a step behind the offender in regards to when and where he will next strike, but it also crosses a number of police boundaries. This ability to gain access to different areas and committing murder makes the task of connecting these offences to the same offender difficult, creating 'linkage blindness' between the various police forces involved. It is arguable that this advantage of being able to access a wider geographical area was one of the reasons why it took so long for the police to finally apprehend Sutcliffe.

Sutcliffe also changed his cars frequently. In police interviews he would often describe which car he had used when committing each murder, and on many occasions it would be different from the one used in the previous offence. For example, Sutcliffe mentions that during the period in which he killed Irene Richardson, he drove either a white or red Corsair (Sutcliffe later stated that he did not remember which Corsair he was driving the night he killed Irene Richardson) (Bilton, 2003: 696). By the time he attacked and killed Josephine Whitaker, he had changed his car to a black Sunbeam Rapier (p.714); he again changed his car to a Rover 3.5 during the period in which he killed Barbara Leach. This frequent changing of vehicles had two advantages. First, it prevented any potential witnesses from making a connection between Sutcliffe's frequent visits to the red light areas and his offences, as they would often describe a vehicle which they had seen, but which of course Sutcliffe no longer owned. Second, by the end of the investigation the police had started to use a basic computer that was thereafter "spewing out ever-increasing numbers of motor vehicles spotted in the red light districts" (p. 394) and which effectively led to information overload.

Whilst Peter Sutcliffe is known to have picked up his victims prior to murdering them outside of his work related activities, he appeared to "educate" himself with regards to suitable hunting grounds and even the selection of victims he would later return to after finishing work:

> "Before Yvonne was found I had committed another murder in Huddersfield Helen Rytka. I did not know the Huddersfield red light area but one day I had to make a delivery in Huddersfield in the afternoon, I noticed a few girls plying for trade near the Market Area. Two or three nights later I decided to pay them a visit. The urge inside me to kill girls was now practically uncontrollable I drove to Huddersfield in my Red Corsair one Evening." (Bilton, 2003: 710)

Due to Sutcliffe's occupations often requiring him to travel over a large geographical space in order to, as Sutcliffe states, "make deliveries", his awareness and activity space would also increase—with the serial murderer gaining more intimate knowledge of various towns and cities that he otherwise would not have had to visit. So, whilst he was officially in these locations fulfilling the requirements given to him by his occupation, Sutcliffe was in fact taking in his surroundings for when he would later dis-engage from his normal day-to-day activities, and then begin to engage in his offending behaviour.

When engaging in his offending behaviour, Sutcliffe evidently used this prior knowledge gained during the course of his occupation to quickly and efficiently return to these previously selected hunting locations that he would otherwise be unaware of. This is further reinforced in Sutcliffe's account of his murders in Leeds, with the serial murderer stating that "I drove off Lumb Lane into church Lane I knew this was a prostitute area" (p. 696). Taking the above into consideration, it is evident that Sutcliffe's occupation brought him within close proximity to those individuals whom he repeatedly targeted and, as a result, informed him of the exact locations in which to return when actively engaging in his offending. Sutcliffe, which records show "worked for Bradford-based T & WH Clark (Holdings) Ltd as a lorry driver delivering goods to and from a number of Black Country destinations" (*Birmingham Mail*, 2014), would have gained extensive knowledge of Britain's road networks including the M1 and routes across the Midlands, may have also been able to use this occupationally gained information in order to return home quickly after each successive murder. For example, Sutcliffe would often note that he would "drive straight home" (p. 695) after murdering his victims and, on some occasions, would describe the exact route that he took when leaving the crime scene:

> "I remember that I backed out of the street into Bowling Back Lane facing towards the city. I drove along Bowling Back Lane towards the general direction of the city centre and drove home to Garden Lane".
> (Bilton, 2003: 702)

Taking the above quote into consideration, it is evident that not only did Sutcliffe's occupation offer him with the ability to gain intimate knowledge of where his victims were located, it also provided him with an extensive knowledge of the road networks—affording him the means to return home over a short period of time.

Key Terms — Awareness and Activity Space

These key terms stem from Crime Pattern Theory. According to this theory, crime occurs when the activity space of a victim overlaps with the activity space of an offender. A person's activity space is comprised of locations in everyday life, for example their place of residence, work, shops, and entertainment areas.

In continuing this examining of how Sutcliffe's occupation may have "taught" him particular skills or traits that would "seep" into his offending, we will now focus on his occupationally oriented mechanic skills. Sutcliffe, who spent many hours in his garage fixing and tweaking his cars (Bilton, 2003, p. 716), would have known this small, private space, in great detail and thus knew the best place to position his weapon(s) for concealment, yet also for easy access. Sutcliffe describes in his formal statement how he would position certain weapons, which also happened to be work tools, in his car:

> "I had picked up the hammer which I had put near my seat for that purpose ... I had taken the screwdriver with the hammer in the well of the driving seat ... I put the hammer and screwdriver on the car floor and drove away." (p. 695)

While he was "working on" (p. 716) his cars, Sutcliffe not only made changes in order to improve the performance of his vehicles, but he also made adaptations that would ultimately improve his own performance when committing murder. Similar to how he would "pull engines out" (p. 748) and replace them in order for his car to perform better, placing his hammer tactfully and discreetly under his seat would have resulted in Sutcliffe being more efficient in attacking his victims and gave him an element of surprise. What we are seeing here is Sutcliffe's "fantasy" space interacting with his physical space, altering his perceived reality in order to successfully fulfil his fantasies and desires (Wilson and Jones, 2008). This observation begins to take the case study out of the realm of the physical, and ventures into the psychological.

A car for Sutcliffe was not only a means to physically escape the scene of his crimes, but also a psychological "refuge". Here we need to consider the note found within one of Sutcliffe's work vehicles presented at the beginning of this case study. Of course, it may simply be that he happened to be in his work vehicle whilst writing, but Sutcliffe's choice of words, including an emphasis on the location in which he wrote this note: his "truck"; suggests a deep rooted psychological connection with his vehicles. It offered him a place of comfort and, more importantly, time. He used this time to think and rationalise what he had done after committing an offence, while also emotionally (as well as physically) removing himself from the crime he had recently committed.

The importance of this space is most apparent when he describes returning to his car after killing his victims. Sutcliffe repeated the phrase "I jumped into my car" (p. 704) on a number of occasions, emphasising the importance of his car as a "refuge" for him to emotionally detach himself from what he had just done. In each of his accounts of what he did after he committed murder Sutcliffe never faile- to mention that he would return to his car. This unwavering narrative in each of his offences implies a deep rooted and psychological connection to his car. The significance of this personal space as a "refuge" for Sutcliffe is developed further during the police interviews:

Q (Police)—"Were there some other occasions when other people were sat in your car whilst you went off and attacked women?"

A (Sutcliffe)—"No, only those two occasions with BIRDSALL." (p. 742)

The two occasions Sutcliffe is referring to with his friend Trevor Birdsall resulted in the assault, but not the death of two women. Sutcliffe not only became aware of the practical complications of attacking women with an unaware accomplice and witness, but also became aware of another issue. For him to be able to successfully transform his mental state from the "normal", socially acceptable personality that his friends and wife knew, to a man capable of committing murder, required a more private space in which Sutcliffe felt comfortable—such as in his car. One of the psychological outcomes of being alone in this place of "refuge" is that he had a private world in which to fantasise about his deepest and most secretive desires; a place where his "latent genius", as he describes in his poem, could be "unleashed". Upon first inspection, Sutcliffe appears to describe such moments with ambiguity and a sense that he is not in control of these thoughts:

> "I felt an inner compulsion to kill a prostitute…i couldn't even bear to go through the motions of having sex with her…i wanted to do what I'd got in my mind as soon as possible." (p. 694)

Sutcliffe does not go into detail about his thoughts and fantasies perhaps because he did not want to share his most intimate desires with others. However, despite his resistance to describing these fantasies, there is a recurring theme in each instance he describes his "inner compulsion" taking over—he was always in a vehicle. For Sutcliffe, his car was his "own world", a place where he felt safe and capable of thinking, dreaming, imagining and fantasising without fear of constraint from normality or reprimand from the real world. In his car or lorry Sutcliffe's fantasy space and physical space became intertwined. They were not only his safe haven in order to escape the realities of everyday life, but also acted as triggers for igniting his latent fantasises. In this respect Sutcliffe was "driving under the influence", though instead of alcohol he was overwhelmed by a feeling of freedom and power. He was able to travel anywhere he wished and his fantasies became his secret passenger.

Sutcliffe not only consciously chose jobs that required practical skills that required him to work with objects, but also a work environment that allowed him to be alone and away from outside interference and managerial oversight. When this ability to be alone with his thoughts and fantasies was interrupted, Sutcliffe stated that he was "deeply upset" (p. 730). During one of his police interviews, he explained how he couldn't "concentrate at work" due to working with an assistant who "didn't fully understand the mechanics of the job". As a result Sutcliffe was consequently demoted and "got a steady number at the Waterworks base at Gilstead". What is interesting here is that Sutcliffe did not appear to be emotionally upset by the fact that he was demoted and ultimately lost responsibility over other individuals. It could be argued that due to the pressures of working with others, especially those with less experience than him, Sutcliffe was losing the freedom that originally attracted him to the job. Being demoted and his choice of the word "steady" to describe his new position, implies a renewed freedom in relation to his work. As a consequence, Sutcliffe is again able to return to his private world and his fantasies.

During his time at the Water Board as a mechanic and later a lorry driver, Sutcliffe was required to be around vehicles, with a shift between working on them as a mechanic, to being inside them as a driver. Vehicles had significance for Sutcliffe, further reinforced by his comments in his formal statement about talking to one of his victims prior to killing her:

> "I asked if she had considered learning to drive I think she said she rode a horse and that it was a satisfactory form of transport." (p. 715)

Comments such as these, though seemingly irrelevant, depict just how much driving meant to Sutcliffe and its role in shaping his occupational choice.

These psychological motivations notwithstanding, it was probably not until he began attacking women that he realised the instrumental advantages of his chosen profession. The most prominent advantage for Sutcliffe was that it offered him a legitimate reason for being in the location that the Ripper was picking up his victims (p. 743). Sutcliffe also later became aware of the advantage of using a different vehicle for work and a different vehicle while off-work, stating in his formal statement that:

> "One day I had to make a delivery in Huddersfield in the afternoon. I noticed a few girls plying for trade near the market area. Two or three nights later I decided to pay them a visit." (p. 710)

For Sutcliffe, his occupation not only gave him a valid reason to be in a particular location, but it also provided camouflage while he scouted the area looking for potential victims. His occupational choice strengthens both the instrumental themes of confusion with regard to any potential eye-witnesses, and the concept of being "above suspicion". With access to both his work vehicle and own car, Sutcliffe was thus capable of confusing both witnesses and police with visits to the red light district masked behind different vehicles.

As discussed previously in this chapter, Peter Sutcliffe's occupation as a lorry driver brought him within close proximity of his target group but unlike, for example, Robert Black, who took direct advantage of a similar occupationally generated proximity, Sutcliffe committed his murders after his work-related activities were finished.

While both men were sexually motivated, the first, and most apparent difference is the particular type of victim targeted by Sutcliffe. For Black, whose occupation took him to smaller and more rural locations, his preference for young girls would likely prevent him from finding a suitable target at night, when parents would arguably not allow their children to walk alone in public. For Sutcliffe, though, who targeted predominantly sex workers, the evening and after dark would be a more suitable time frame in which to successfully commit an offence.

When applying rational choice theory, in which it argued that offenders weigh up the perceived benefits and risks to committing a crime, it would arguably be perceived by Sutcliffe as advantageous to attempt to target and select victims at night, as stopping and picking up sex workers in a highly recognisable work lorry in the day may increase the risks of being identified and apprehended much sooner. Sutcliffe also lacked the extensive occupational freedom that was afforded to Black, with Sutcliffe actually having to manage others at a time (Bilton, 2003)—this may have further prevented in him from engaging in criminal behaviour whilst supposedly undertaking work-related activities. So, whilst Sutcliffe held an occupation which provided him with close proximity with his preferred target group, the type of victim he targeted and the more managerial controlled nature of his employment may have contributed to him not taking immediate advantage of the proximity his work, on occasion, provided.

Key Term — Rational Choice Theory

Originating from the Administrative School of Criminology, rational choice theory adopts the utilitarian idea that humans are reasoning actors who weigh up the means and ends, and the costs and benefits, and as a result make a rational choice

Chapter Four presented a comprehensive analysis of each known British serial killer with regard to their occupational background. Occupations that involve long periods of isolation, coupled with driving, are most common for these particular offenders. Through the implementation of a case study, we have also identified the unique traits that transient serial killers may possess that differentiate them from other categories of serial killers. We have sought to demonstrate the instrumental and psychological shift that a mobile serial killer may go through when committing his crimes. Instrumentally it encompasses the practical advantages of using a vehicle, including such factors as a quick and efficient "getaway"; access to a wider geographical area; and the ability to find suitable areas in order to attack, or dispose of the victim. There is also an opportunity to confuse any witnesses, or the police by changing vehicles on a regular basis, and by selecting vehicles that will improve their status on the road and elevate them to being "above suspicion". Weapons can also be hidden in their vehicles. Finally, the vehicle also offers the offender a wealth of options in order to keep up their pretence ensuring that their victim is unaware and cooperative for as long as possible.

Revision

- What type of victim did Sutcliffe repeatedly target?
- What time of day did he engage in his offending?
- Did his occupation influence this at all? Where there perhaps other factors at play?
- What were the "instrumental" advantages that Sutcliffe's occupation and vehicle provided him in relation to his crimes?
- In what ways may have Sutcliffe's occupation and vehicle impact him psychologically in relation to his crimes?

Further Reading

For more information of the Yorkshire Ripper case M Bilton's (2003), *Wicked Beyond Belief: The Hunt for the Yorkshire Ripper*, London: Harperpress offers one of the most comprehensive accounts of the investigation, including the transcription of Sutcliffe's confession and subsequent police interviews. R Cross (1981), *The Yorkshire Ripper*, London: Dell Pub. Co and Gordon Burn (1984), *Somebody's Husband, Somebody's Son: The Story of the Yorkshire Ripper,* London: Heinemann also offer an in-depth account of the five-year hunt for Sutcliffe. This chapter briefly touched upon the rather specific type of victim Sutcliffe targeted; D Wilson's (2007), *Serial Killers: Hunting Britons and Their Victims, 1960 to 2006,* Winchester: Waterside Press expands upon this in much more detail, offering a sociological perspective as to why sex workers were so frequently murdered. R Keppel and W Birnes (2003), *The Psychology of Serial Killer Investigations: The Grisly Business Unit,* London: Academic Press takes a very different approach in analysing this particular case of serial murder, with the authors instead focusing on the investigation itself, and why it took five years before Sutcliffe was finally apprehended.

THE FEMALE SERIAL KILLER 7

> ...the notion of a female serial killer has not entered our popular consciousness of fear or into our alarmed imaginations in the same menacing way that the figure of the male serial killer has. Women serial killers seem to border on the comic or titillating for many of us. Compare the monikers we give male serial killers (Jack the Ripper, Boston Strangler, Night Stalker, Skid Row Slasher, Bedroom Basher, Slavemaster) with the female ones (Lady Bluebeard, Giggling Grandma, Lonely Hearts Killer, Lady Rotten, Black Widow, Angel of Death, Barbie Killer, Death Row Granny). We have not been taking female serial killers seriously enough...
>
> Peter Vronskey, 2007.

Introduction — Crime, Violence, Sex and Gender

Research into serial killing has tended to focus largely upon male perpetrators, who are indeed responsible for around 85 per cent of these crimes. In a British context, the 20th-century has seen only three female serial killers, two of whom committed their crimes with a male partner — see *Box 1: British Female Serial Killers in the 20th-century*. This 'maleness' is not restricted to serial killing but is echoed in crime more broadly and is a starting point for understanding why we hear much less about crime committed by women — serial killings included — than we do about crime committed by men.

Consider for example recent data for England and Wales — which reported that 90 per cent of homicide suspects were men and in 81 per cent of all recorded violent incidents, the offender was male. Sex differences not only relate to the crimes themselves but also to the wider criminal justice system — fewer than one in five arrests recorded by the police involve women and men represent 95.2 per cent of the overall prison population.

Box 1: British Female Serial Killers in the 20th-century

Myra Hindley

Hindley and her partner, Ian Brady, killed at least five (perhaps as many as ten) children and young people between 1963 and 1965 in the North of England. Hindley was 21-years-of-age when the first murder for which she was convicted took place. The homicides were believed to be sexually motivated and the method of killing varied, including strangulation, stabbing, shooting and torture. Brady and Hindley were convicted of five murders in 1966 and each received sentences of life in prison.

Rosemary West

West and her husband, Frederick, killed at least ten girls and young women in the South-West of England between 1971 and 1987. The victims included young women who were lodging at their home, their children and Frederick's former partner. The killings were believed to be sexually motivated. The Wests were arrested and charged with murder in 1994—Frederick committed suicide whilst awaiting trial but Rosemary went on to be convicted of ten murders, resulting in a life sentence.

Beverley Allitt

Beverley Allitt, the only 20th-century British female serial killer to kill alone, killed four children whilst working as a nurse in the East of England in 1994. She injected most of her victims with potassium and insulin, suffocating a further victim. Allitt was found to have Munchausen Syndrome by Proxy—which involves harming others to elicit attention for oneself. Allitt was found guilty of four murders, three attempted murders and six counts of grievous bodily harm. She received 13 life sentences, which she is currently serving at Rampton Secure Hospital in England.

So in relation to the nature and extent of offending and in terms of criminal justice outcomes there are clear differences between men and women. If we were looking solely at statistical probability, given the relatively even split between men and women as proportions of the population, we might expect that they would each commit around 50 per cent of crime and our prisons would be filled with roughly equal numbers of male and female prisoners. So why is this not the case? What is going on here?

The answer is a complex one but it essentially involves examining the roles that men and women occupy in society. Here we are looking beyond sex—the biological distinction between a male and a female—to encompass gender, which is associated with social expectations around how men and women should behave. These expectations are embodied in masculine and feminine traits and characteristics (see *Box 2: Feminine and Masculine Traits and Characteristics*) which are informed by socially constructed norms, values, attitudes and beliefs. By socially constructed we mean that these things do not just exist—they have been learned and shared within and between social groups—in other words, they are cultural. As such, criminologists often describe the social issues they study as **gendered** (see *Key Term—Gendered*). However, it is important to remember that gender is but one **social division** (see *Key Term—Social Divisions*), other examples are age, social class, ethnicity and disability, all of which overlap and influence the nature of individual and group experiences of the social world.

Box 2: Feminine and Masculine Traits and Characteristics

FEMININITY	MASCULINITY
Emotional	Rational
Passive	Active
Dependent	Independent
Content	Ambitious
Cooperative	Competitive
Sex object	Sexually aggressive
Sensitive	Insensitive
Intuitive	Analytical
Selfless, altruistic	Selfish, purposeful
Carer / nurturer	Provider

Key Term — Gendered

We might describe an issue as a gendered issue when there is variation in the way it is experienced by men and women and / or when the response to the issue is different when it is discussed in relation to men or women. For example, parenthood is a gendered issued because there is considerable variation in expectations placed upon men and women in their roles as parents and how men and women experience parenthood.

There has been a plethora of legislation and policy initiatives from the early 20th-century, which have aimed to tackle gender divisions in various contexts — for example the 1970 Equal Pay Act and 1975 Sex Discrimination Act (now enshrined in the Equality Act 2010). However, whilst some groups of women now have a broader range of choices as a result of such changes, others do not. For these women, we could argue that the intersection of various elements of their social identity creates a less favourable set of social circumstances for their lives. So when we study female serial killers — particularly from a structural perspective — we need to remember that their gender is important but it is just one part of the larger jigsaw. They are not "just women" but women who belong to particular age groups, social classes and ethnic groups to name but a few elements of their social identities. However, we will see that interpretations of female serial killers can be heavily gendered — fatal violence has a much easier fit with masculinity than it does with femininity and, given this, we are much more likely to expect women to play the role of the victim rather than the aggressor.

To Kill …

As a society, we have trouble making sense of women who kill once. When we turn to examine women who kill multiple times, we become considerably challenged. It is worth considering the former group prior to examining female serial killers both in terms of who these women and victims are and in relation to how we have attempted to make sense of their actions.

Key Term — Social Divisions

"... when we talk about social divisions, we mean those substantial differences between people that run throughout our society. A social division has at least two categories, each of which has distinctive cultural and material features. In other words, one category is better positioned than the other, and has a better share of resources because it has greater power over the way our society is organized ..." (Payne, 2000: 2).

Writing about the UK, Brookman (2005) argues that women who kill once tend to do so within a domestic context, their victim more often than not being their intimate male partner or their child. In terms of socio-demographics, the perpetrators are often aged 25–40, with below average educational attainment, unemployed and experiencing economic deprivation. Indeed, around 80 per cent of victims are family members, and 40–45 per cent of women who kill will murder their own children, with about one-third killing their male partner. Examining cases from the US, Mann (1996) comes to similar conclusions, identifying single, African-American mothers with a median age of 31 and a below high-school level of education as the typical perpetrator.

These women tend to live in households where domestic abuse is entrenched, may have childhood experiences of similar trauma, misuse drugs and / or alcohol, and lack formal and informal sources of support—in short their circumstances are characterised by "sheer desperation" (Brookman, 2005). In killing their child or partner, these women clearly deviate from the carer / nurturer feminine role noted in *Box 2*. However, we frame their violence in a gendered way and reclaim them as women by casting them in the role of the victim, *driven* to commit their crimes through helplessness and desperation—emphasising the emotional and dependent feminine elements of their identities. We view their crimes as a reaction to circumstances in which their choices are heavily restricted by the way in which their gender has intersected with other social factors. Such an interpretation enables us to make sense of some women who kill within our existing frames of reference around gender and femininity. However, in the absence of such factors, we adopt a different approach to understanding them. D'Cruze *et al* (2006) discuss the role of the media in making sense of those we are unable to re-feminise. In presenting their cases to viewers and readers, the media must compress complex events and circumstances into easily recognisable, accessible narratives such as 'evil' or 'bad'. They explain that a woman committing extreme violence can be presented as far more evil than a male killer. If she cannot be recuperated as a powerless, debilitated victim, the social threat that a murdering woman poses is often dealt with by "outlawing" her symbolically from the social order through narrative strategies of demonisation. (D'Cruze *et al*, 2006, p. 48).

...and Kill Again

Turning to examine women who kill more than once. Schechter and Schechter (2010) argue that that they tend to kill in certain kinds of ways (either indirectly, through their partners, or covertly, via poisoning or smothering); choose similar victims (their own children, their unsuspecting husbands, their elderly charges, their ailing patients), and victims with whom they have a certain kind of personal relationship. There has been other academic support for these propositions, with estimates that nearly three-quarters of female serial killers poisoned their victims, most of whom were people close to them—family, friends or acquaintances—in only 10 per cent of cases was the victim a stranger. Hickey (2006) describes the typical offender as largely white (95 per cent), with very little in the way of a criminal record and 31-years-of-age on average when she began killing. This suggests that female serial killers may not be multiply disadvantaged to the same extent as women who kill once—as such, we have difficulties in casting them in the role of the powerless victim and revert to demonisation, labelling them as evil monsters (D'Cruze *et al*, 2006).

Kelleher and Kelleher (1998) produced the only typology to focus specifically upon female serial killers[1]. They identified nine types of female serial killer based on their research into around 100 cases, around half of which were from the US. The impetus to develop the typology came from their view that the organized / disorganized dichotomy developed by The FBI's Robert Ressler discussed in *Chapter Two* was not sufficiently helpful in understanding female serial killers. Seven[2] of Kelleher and Kelleher's types are summarised in *Table 1*.

As stated previously, this typology is the only one that was developed specifically for women, therefore it is highly cited in academic enquiry into women who commit serial murder. However, if we are trying to draw conclusions or make generalisations about women who commit serial homicide, we do not have a particularly easy job on our hands—indeed—female serial killers appear to be characterised by their diversity than their homogeneity. We could though state with a reasonable degree of confidence that these women do not embody the characteristics of those who commit a single murder in that their circumstances do not appear to be characterised by domestic abuse or a sense of hopelessness—and as stated earlier, this may go some way to explaining the evil or monster labels drawn upon in representations of these women in popular culture.

1. It is however worth noting that other scholars have offered typologies, but these have not been based solely upon female serial killers. For example, Holmes and Holmes (1994, 1998) built upon their typology of male serial killers to encompass female offenders. However, as Farrell *et al* (2013) point out, there are some key criticisms of this typology. Firstly, it is based on a typology of male offenders and may include assumptions that do not appreciate the gendered nature of women's violence. Secondly, the authors do not provide details of any sample used in developing the typology—we simply do not know the real cases that have informed it and as such are limited in our ability to make judgements about its generalisability. Thirdly, Schurman-Kauflin (2000) suggests that the typology is over-simplistic and as such it is difficult to apply it to cases where the offender has more than one motivation.
2. There were a total of nine categories in Kelleher and Kelleher's original typology—the two others were "Unexplained" and "Unsolved". They have been excluded from this chapter as they refer respectively to killings for which a reason or motive cannot be established and unsolved cases where it is thought that the killer is a woman. We do not feel that these categories are particularly useful—rather they are "holding pens" for cases where insufficient information was available to come to a conclusion.

However, it appears to be easier to describe female serial killers by what they are *not* rather than what they are! This is a view shared by Farrell *et al* (2013), who argue that "existing classification systems for these rare offenders are inadequate" (p. 269), including Kelleher and Kelleher (1998) within this description. Indeed, they have highlighted several issues with the typology, which we outline below alongside our own reservations.

Table 1: Kelleher and Kelleher's Typology of Female Serial Killers

Type	Description	Example
Black Widow	Kills multiple husbands, partners or other family members. May also kill victims outside of the family with whom she has developed a personal relationship. Begins killing after age of 25. Kills for at least ten years before being apprehended. Victim count six to 13. Poisoning is her most common method. Motives are diverse and may encompass profit or crime.	Belle Gunness Active between 1896 and 1908, first killed at age 37. Estimated to have killed between 16 and 49 victims—husbands, children and workers. Used poison and killed most victims for life insurance proceeds or to obtain their assets.
Angel of Death	Kills physically vulnerable individuals who are involuntarily dependent upon her care in an institutional setting (e.g. hospitals or nursing homes). Motives include desire to control others and a need for recognition and self-aggrandisement through efforts to 'save' some victims. May have an undiagnosed psychological disorder (e.g. Munchausen Syndrome by Proxy). Kills adult victims by lethal injection of substances available in the workplace and may supplement this method with suffocation when killing children. Difficult to establish number of victims given the normality of death in the killing environment but estimated that she will kill at least eight before being apprehended. Potential mobility between institutions may lead to a longer killing period or prevent detection altogether.	Genene Jones Active between 1978 and 1982, first killed at age 27. Responsible for at least eleven homicides—babies and children in her care whilst working as a nurse. Killed her victims through lethal injection (typically digoxin), motive believed to be egotistical, involving elements of power and control.

Type	Description	Example
Sexual Predator	Kills others in clear acts of sexual homicide. Motive is sexual in nature[3].	Aileen Wuornos Active between 1989 and 1990, first homicide committed at age 33. Killed at least seven men whilst working as a prostitute in Florida. Shot her victims with a .22 pistol. Motive believed to be sexual—connected to her prostitution.
Revenge	Kills in revenge against an individual or entity. Killing is in response to overwhelming sense of rejection or abandonment. Victims are symbolic of or responsible for her affront. Victims often include members of her own family. Poisons or suffocates victims. Kills three or four victims over a period of two years or less. Claims first victim when in her 20s. Rare—emotional characteristics relating to revenge do not often translate into sustainable aggression.	Martha Ann Johnson Active between 1977 and 1982, aged 22 when she committed her first homicide. Her victims were four of her children, all killed following arguments with her husband. Johnson suffocated them by rolling onto them as they slept—she weighed around 17 stones.
Profit or Crime	Kills clearly for financial gain, victims are not members of her own family. Driven by greed, killing is akin to a career to generate income beyond her needs. Organized, intelligent and resourceful. Over 25 when she commits her first murder. Claims between five and ten victims during a killing period between five and ten years. Poisons her victims. Likely to be apprehended sooner than the Black Widow as she kills in a local area, she is not a mobile killer.	Dorothea Puente Active between 1986 and 1988, committed her first homicide aged 57. Puente killed individuals who lodged at her home and continued to obtain their social security benefits after they had died. Killed between nine and 25 people, using poison as her weapon.

3. Note that Kelleher and Kelleher (1998) describe features of the Aileen Wuornos case in relation to this type—as such they do not make further generalisations beyond the sexual motivation. They do however make reference to the case of Marti Enriquetta—a Spanish woman apprehended in 1912 for killing six children—she tortured and sexually abused her victims and engaged in acts of cannibalism with their bodies. The killings had ritualistic elements to them, involving boiling her victims' bodies in water.

Type	Description	Example
Team Killer	Systematically kills others or participates in their killings in conjunction with another person or people. Teams can be male/female, all female or family in composition. Female members are aged 20–25 when they commit their first killing, are active for one to two years (there tends to be an unstable relationship between partners) and claim between nine and 15 victims. There is usually a dominant individual. Motives vary depending on team composition—e.g. male/female tends to be sexually motivated.	Charlene Gallego Active between 1978 and 1980, Gallego was part of a killing team with her husband, Gerald. Charlene was aged 22 at the time of the first homicide, the Gallegos killed ten young women, whom they held hostage and sexually brutalised before bludgeoning or shooting them.
Question of Sanity	Kills others but is incapable of understanding the meaning or impact of her actions. Majority of these cases involve an Angel of Death serial killer. Rare because serial murder by its very nature involves calculation and planning—and therefore perpetrators are largely found to be fully culpable for their actions.	Bobbie Sue Terrell In 1984, Terrell is believed to have killed 12 people by lethal injection in a period of less than two weeks. She was 29-years-of-age at the time of the homicides, her victims were elderly patients in the nursing home where she worked. Terrell had a history of schizophrenia and Munchausen Syndrome.

Source: Adapted from Kelleher and Kelleher, 1998, p. 11.

The descriptions and criteria for each of Kelleher and Kelleher's types are variable in that some include age ranges, offence-related information and length of killing periods—whilst others only include some of these variables. Related to this, it is challenging to establish exactly what cases the typology was based on—nowhere do Kelleher and Kelleher provide a comprehensive breakdown of which women fall into which category (or categories—as the typology is clearly not mutually exclusive). A further key issue is that the typology builds upon the idea of motive—focusing as a central point upon *why* these women committed serial homicide and using that as the starting point to build the typology.

This may be problematic because of what we know about gender from the introductory section of this chapter. In answering the "Why?" question, how can we be sure that Kelleher and Kelleher's reasoning was not gendered? How do we know that socially constructed ideas about femininity and womanhood did not influence the formation of these categories? The presence of an "unexplained" category is also concerning, both to us and others given the vague and catch-all nature of such a category. So too some academics have to apply Kelleher and Kelleher's typology to a sample of 70 female serial killers who were included in the original study. For example, Farrell *et al* have done so although they excluded team killers from their analysis of the cases—arguing that they differed from solo female serial killers because their motivations were intertwined with those of their partner, making it challenging to attribute a particular motive specifically to them. Drawing upon information contained in newspaper articles relating to the cases, Farrell *et al* noted that in 56 per cent of the homicides they reanalysed, the killings were driven by a combination of the Kelleher and Kelleher motives—a point they illustrate with reference to the crimes of Tillie Klimek,

> "The crimes of Tillie Klimek exemplify the multiple motivations that can be attributed to a series of murders committed by a female offender. She profited from the deaths of her three husbands, which meets Kelleher and Kelleher's criteria for a Black Widow. However, profit accounted for motive in only three of the eight deaths to which she is connected. It is suspected that she murdered her boyfriend John Guszkowski after he attempted to terminate their relationship, and she was suspected of murdering the three children of an aunt with whom she had a disagreement. The murders of Guszkowski and the Zakrzewski children appear to have been motivated by revenge or anger, although Guszkowski's murder would be atypical of this classification because the offender murdered the object of her anger. Revenge was also cited as the motivation in the murder of Klimek's cousin Rose Chudzinskey when the offender poisoned her dinner following an argument." (Farrell *et al*, 2013: 283)

All of this may suggest that focusing so heavily upon motive may not provide answers to be able to categorise all female serial killers. Indeed, Farrell *at al* argue in relation to categorising female serial killers based on motive, "these women, and their crimes, defy our need to label them and neatly classify their actions" (p. 284). However, Farrell *et al* (2013) do suggest a starting point that they emphasise will require further research,

> "...it may be possible to broadly categorise female serial murderers into two groups, although this dichotomy may not be as applicable with male offenders. The occupational female serial murderer meets, targets, and gains access to her victims through her career, whereas the hearthside female serial murderer interacts and accesses victims through personal contact...Jane Toppan, Aileen Wuornos and Genene Jones would then fall within the parameters of occupational offenders, whereas offenders such as Judi Buenoano, Nannie Doss, Audrey Marie Hilley, Martha Johnson, Tillie Klimek, Louise Vermilyea and Stella Williamson would be considered hearthside offenders." (Farrell *et al,* 2013, p. 285)

We believe that this is a promising approach. Most of what we know about female serial killers for the moment is rather descriptive, focusing upon their individual biographies and personal characteristics. This is of course to be expected, when a field of study is in its early stages it must first focus upon identifying and describing the phenomenon under investigation, getting a feel for what it "looks like" but in so doing, existing typologies tended to adopt a medico-psychological approach. However, in identifying the social institutions of economy and family as the backdrop for their crimes through the suggested occupational and hearthside categories, and noting the gendered differential nature of men's and women's experiences, Farrell *et al* (2013) are pushing this field of study into a more structural domain, moving away from the medico-psychological approach by emphasising the social, historical and cultural context of these crimes.

Progressing the Study of Female Serial Killers—The 'Institutional' Approach

The key to furthering the structural approach to female (and indeed male) serial killers may lie within more established theoretical and conceptual frameworks within the social sciences—notably the *institutional* approach.

Messner and Rosenfeld (2004) define institutions as systems of rules governing the operation of social positions, the roles connected to them and the organizations in which roles are enacted and goals are achieved. Indeed, in relation to making sense of crime, Rosenfeld argues "All of criminology would be better off if greater attention were devoted to the big picture—the relationship between crime and the interplay of institutions in the social systems of whole societies" (2011, p. 1). The word "institution" therefore encompasses: *structures* such as the polity (or political system), economy, education, family and religion; *organizations* like schools, businesses, charities and faith based organizations; and *roles* including mother, father, worker, student, volunteer. The institutional approach aims to identify how institutions shape and influence the social world and the individuals that inhabit it. Criminologists who adopt an institutional approach argue that there is a dynamic, two-way relationship between individuals and institutions—institutions influence individuals and vice-versa. Embedded within this process are cultural factors such as values, beliefs, norms and imbalances of power. Further exploring how the two-way relationship between individuals and institutions works, Hall and Taylor (1996) argue that institutions provide blueprints or road maps for social action,

> "...when faced with a situation, the individual must find a way of recognizing it as well as responding to it, and the scripts or templates implicit in the institutional world provide the means for accomplishing both of these tasks...the individual works and reworks the available institutional templates to devise a course of action." (pp. 948–949)

Exploring this further, March and Olsen (1989) talk about the *logic of appropriateness,* whereby individuals think about what action to take and in so doing, consider the extent to which different courses of action would be socially acceptable or unacceptable. In making their decisions, not all individuals will have exactly the same range of choices —as their decision-making takes place within the boundaries of what is "normal" for them. So for example, in deciding whether or not to go to university, the student from a wealthy middle-class family with siblings and parents who have all had a university education will have a different "normal" to the student from a poorer background, whose parents and siblings all went straight to work upon leaving school.

It is possible that the institutional approach may shed new light upon female serial killers that will help us better develop the motive-centred typologies. We argue that an institutional analysis of female serial killers should pose the following questions:

What structures are central to / peripheral to / absent from her life (polity, education, religion, economy, family)?

- What were the individual circumstances and wider social context in which the killing took place? What was the killer's social identity (social class, age, ethnicity, disability)? What social roles did she occupy (worker, mother, partner, student)?
- What were the 'rules of the game'—how should she have been interacting with the institutional landscape through her social roles? For example, as a middle-class girl from a good school—was she expected to go to university?
- To what extent did the female serial killer conform to the rules? For example was she a "conscientious student", an "educational achiever"?
- To what extent did the usual rewards for conforming to the rules (or punishments for breaking the rules) affect her behaviour? For example, did the potential reward of getting a good job or the risk of being unemployed cause her commit to her studies?

- Did adhering to or breaking the rules result in the expected outcomes for her? For example, by being a "conscientious student", did she get a degree and a graduate job?
- What was being achieved by killing? What did she get from it? How can we make sense of what she did by considering her relationship with the institutional landscape?

The phenomenon of female serial murder remains a complex web, which criminologists are only just beginning to unpick and indeed as the enquiry into female serial murder is relatively new, there exists considerable potential for approaching this topic in a creative way. In the next chapter, we apply the institutional approach to the analysis of Mary Ann Cotton, a 19th-century British female serial killer.

Revision

- What proportion of serial killings are committed by women?
- Why is there not an equal split between the proportion of violent crimes committed by men and those committed by women?
- How do female serial killers differ from women who kill only once?
- Name the seven types of female serial killer identified by Kelleher and Kelleher (1998)—what are the problems with this typology?
- What do we mean by an 'institutional' approach?

Further Reading

Several texts are cited throughout this chapter, which will be helpful in developing a deeper understanding of the concepts we have explored in it. For those who are interested in finding out more about existing typologies, we would advise reading the full versions of R M Homes and J E De Burger (1988), *Serial Murder,* Newbury Park, CA: Sage. Those interested in exploring individual cases of female serial killers in more detail will find Vronsky (2007), *Female Serial*

Killers: How and Why Women Become Monsters, London: Penguin a useful starting point and an earlier book by M D Kelleher and C L Kelleher (1998), *Murder Most Rare: The Female Serial Killer*, Westport, CT: Praeger. We also cited A L Farrell, R D Keppel and V Tittering-ton (2011), 'Lethal Ladies: Revisiting what we know about female serial murderers', *Homicide Studies,* 15/3: 228–252; E Schechter and H Schechter (2010), 'Killing with Kindness: Nature, Nurture, and the Female Serial Killer,' in S Waller (ed.) *Serial Killers: Philosophy for Everyone,* pp.117–128. Oxford: Wiley-Blackwell and S D'Cruze, S Walklate and S Pegg (2006), *Murder*, Cullompton: Willan. Other references can be found within these books and articles.

MARY ANN COTTON

8

> A woman, still comparatively young, who has formed and enjoyed all the ties which are supposed to humanise the feelings and endear life, who has been a wife and a mother, and who never seems to have been suspected by friends and neighbours of being in any degree different from the vast majority of her sex, has been proved guilty of the cold-blooded and deliberate murder or an innocent child.
>
> *Leeds Mercury*, 8th March 1873

Introduction

Mary Ann Cotton (hereafter known as Mary Ann) is arguably one of the most prolific serial killers but one that few people have ever heard about. She committed her crimes in North-East England in the late 19th-century, systematically murdering 17 people, the majority of whom were family members; three husbands, her lover, her mother, a sister in law, six of her own children and five step-children. The reaction to her crimes was sheer disbelief that a woman was capable of committing such terrible acts and her case turned into something of an urban legend in the North-East—evident in the following nursery rhyme, which could be heard in the streets and playgrounds of the towns and villages where she took the lives of those around her,

> Mary Ann Cotton,
> She's dead and she's rotten,
> She lies in her bed,
> With her eyes wide open.
> Sing, sing, oh, what can I sing,

Mary Ann Cotton is tied up with string,
Where, where? Up in the air,
Sellin' black puddens a penny a pair.

(Traditional)[1]

In this chapter we will examine the crimes of Mary Ann in detail, applying the points about female serial killers that we covered in *Chapter Seven*. Use the case study to think about the typologies offered by Kelleher and Kelleher (1998) and Farrell *et al* (2013). Also, critically reflect upon what an "institutional" approach to her case might tell us as we examine some of the social roles she occupied during her life. We will begin this chapter with an overview of the case.

The Life and Crimes of Mary Ann

Mary Ann was born into a devout Methodist family in 1832 in the small English mining village of Murton. Her father was killed in a pit accident in 1842 and her mother re-married. In 1852, Mary Ann married a 35 year old labourer, William Mowbray. She is known to have had at least four children with Mowbray, all of whom died—two whilst their father was alive. Following Mowbray's death in 1865, one of her two surviving children died and the other was taken in by her mother. Mary Ann moved alone to Sunderland in the summer of 1865 and worked as a nurse in the Sunderland Infirmary, marrying one of her patients—George Ward—later in 1865. No children came of this marriage and Ward died in October 1866.

In November of the same year, Mary Ann began work as a housekeeper for James Robinson, a widower with five children. Within a matter of weeks one of Robinson's sons had died. By February 1867 Mary Ann was pregnant with Robinson's child, but was called away to look after her mother, who was dead within nine days. Within two months of her return, Mary Ann's child (whom her mother had previously cared for) and two more of Robinson's children were dead. Mary Ann and Robinson married in August 1867 and their baby was

1. The origins of this nursery rhyme are described in Wilson, 2013, p. 153.

dead by February of the following year. Following disagreements over money—discussed later—Mary Ann fled from Robinson and abandoned their baby son with a friend—this child would be only one of two children who would outlive his mother.

Mary Ann was then introduced to widower Frederick Cotton by his sister Margaret in early 1870. By the end of March 1870, Margaret was dead. When the Cottons were (bigamously) married in September 1870, Mary Ann was pregnant with Frederick's child, born in January 1871. The couple moved to West Auckland with their baby and two boys from Frederick's previous marriage, one of whom was seven-year-old Charles Edward. Frederick Cotton died suddenly in September 1871. Mary Ann had meanwhile been asked to nurse an excise officer by the name of Quick-Manning and they soon formed a relationship. In the space of three weeks between March and April 1872 two of the children and a lodger were all dead. The only other person at this time left in the household was seven-year-old Charles Edward and it was his death that was to lead to her arrest. Having failed in her attempts to get Charles Edward fostered then admitted to the workhouse, Mary Ann suggested that he would die in a conversation with Thomas Riley—a local overseer of poor relief. Upon learning of Charles Edward's death only days later, Riley called in the police and a subsequent autopsy revealed that the he died of arsenic poisoning. At the time of her arrest on 18 July 1872 Cotton was pregnant. Mary Ann gave birth to the child, a daughter, in prison and was executed in Durham Jail in March 1873.

What 'Type' of Serial Killer was Mary Ann?

In terms of Kelleher and Kelleher's typology, which we critiqued in *Chapter Seven,* what type of serial killer is Mary Ann? At first glance, she would appear to fit into the *Black Widow* category in that she killed husbands, children, other family members and people outside of her family with whom she developed a personal relationship. As Kelleher and Kelleher suggest in relation to the Black Widow, her murders encompassed profit—she benefited financially from life insurance policies she had taken out for some of her victims.

Therefore we could explain her crime solely through the *Black Widow* or *Profit / Crime* motivations. How about the categories suggested by Farrell *et al* (2013), which, to recap are the occupational serial killer, who "meets, targets, and gains access to her victims through her career" and the hearthside serial killer, who "interacts and accesses victims through personal contact" (Farrell *et al*, 2013, p. 285).

We could argue that Mary Ann was both. She could be described as an occupational serial killer as she met George Ward through her work as a nurse and James Robinson through her job as his housekeeper. She could also be described as a hearthside killer as she accessed other victims through her personal contact with them as their mother, step-mother, wife, lover, and sister-in-law. So are these typologies helping us make sense of Mary Ann? Can we say that we really understand why she chose to commit murder time and time again? Not really. At this point we have simply assigned her one or more labels, which may partially explain her motives but what does motive really tell us? Many women may have had similar "motives" or desires during the 19th-century—for example a wish for more money and financial security—but very few of these women went on to systematically murder their relatives to achieve this. Perhaps it is not simply identifying the motive that is important here—perhaps we need to understand where it comes from in the first place and then what makes an individual act on it. So what made Mary Ann different from these other women? Throughout this chapter we will explore a range of explanations for this.

Mary Ann Cotton Through the Lens of the 19th-century Media

It is not just 21st-century criminologists who have difficult in making sense of Mary Ann. The 19th-century also struggled to understand her—which was clearly reflected in the media portrayal of her case at the time. In *Chapter Five* we saw the considerable role of the media in reporting serial murder—magnifying or minimising particular cases and influencing the way in which serial killers are perceived by the public. It is worth considering the role of the media in her case because it casts light on some additional perspectives—in particular the social context within which her crime were committed.

Before we explore how the 19th-century media made sense of Mary Ann it is important to remember that the media of the late-1800s was vastly different from the one we have today. This was a period in which the newspaper began to emerge as a valued and coveted source of information. Indeed, newspapers were the *only* form of media at this time—there was not 24 hour rolling news on television or live updates online.

Coverage of the case in the local press was more extensive than in the national press, which is not particularly surprising as her trial took place in 1872, a time known as the heyday of the provincial newspaper. It is also important to note that 19th-century newspapers were written for and consumed by men, at least until the arrival of the "new journalism" of the late-1800s, in which newspapers took on characteristics of more "feminine" mediums like the magazine. Mary Ann's case arrived a few years prior to the new journalism therefore the main newspaper audience for her trial was largely male and middle-class.

Murder was a particularly popular topic for 19th-century newspapers—criminal trials were mass cultural spectacles and press attention shone a spotlight on the most shocking of murders, particularly those in which the death sentence was a real possibility. When it came to reporting upon women who killed, there were some key differences in the type of coverage by local and national newspapers. Local newspapers were elite, politically conservative and considerably more sympathetic towards the accused than the more liberal national papers aimed at a wider readership and hence more likely to use "shock" value. Local newspapers were often sensitive and understanding in their portrayal of women who killed their own children, sometimes leading petitions to have their death sentences commuted. These were cases where a mother's actions were attributed to harsh social conditions in which the financial pressures created by another mouth to feed would plunge families further into poverty. The 19th-century was a hard time for impoverished families—these were the years before modern welfare and support from the state was very much hit and miss depending upon where you lived. The actions of mothers who killed their children in such circumstances were interpreted altruistically—although they were indeed committing a criminal act, they were perceived as doing so to save their children from miserable lives. Essentially, newspapers would cast these women in the role of the helpless victim rather than the aggressor—something we explored in *Chapter Seven*. However, cases outside of this frame of reference were met with downright condemnation—and Mary Ann was one such woman—the journalists writing about her were unable to place her within the "victim" role.

The *Newcastle Journal*, for example, believed that "the most astounding thought of all is that a woman could act thus without becoming terrible and repulsive" (11 March 1873); the *Times* described Mary Ann as "a comely-looking, gentle-eyed woman" (21 March 1873); and the *Durham County Advertiser* thought that "perhaps the greatest wonder is that a woman could successfully practise for so many years a system of poisoning without betraying her secret" (28 March 1873). It is claimed that newspaper pictures of Mary Ann were deliberately altered to make her appear more frightening, clearly more in keeping with notions of what a murderer would look like. These Victorian journalists were finding it hard to make sense of her as both what we would now call a "serial killer", and as a woman. She was "comely-looking and gentle-eyed", not "terrible and repulsive"; and the "greatest wonder" was that a woman could keep the murders a secret for as long as Mary Ann had done, implying her deviousness and marking her out as different from the mothers who had killed their children in an altruistic manner. Her crimes were considered so exceptional that even her pregnancy and new motherhood during her incarceration, despite attracting some sympathy from the public, only succeeded in postponing her execution rather than resulting in a reprieve.

Those reporting on and reading about Mary Ann's trial came from a rather different, middle-class world to the one that she inhabited. The shock with which her case was received is not altogether surprising as her murderous actions were in distinct contradiction to ideals of 19th-century motherhood. Whilst the media had rallied opinion and succeeded in bringing about reprieves in previous cases in which the death penalty had been handed out to a pregnant woman, this did not occur in Mary Ann's case. However, the fact that she murdered her children was not the sole explanation for the difficulties that the press had in conceptualising her; the fact that she killed her children for reasons that were other than altruistic were sufficient to confuse existing cultural norms which had to some extent come to accept the murder of children in some circumstances.

"But surely there was something wrong with her?" Medical Explanations for Mary Ann Cotton

As described above, Mary Ann defied explanation within 19th-century altruistic frames of reference. But what about other explanations? Medicine was playing an increasingly important role in *explaining* crime in the 19th-century. At a time when criminological theory development was influenced significantly by the biological positivism we discussed in *Chapter Two*, embodied most notably in the contribution of Lombroso. It is perhaps not surprising that this period witnessed the increasing *medicalisation* of women's crime.

Key Term — Medicalisation

Medicalisation occurs when problems or issues that were not previously medical in nature come to be defined and treated as medical problems, usually in terms of illnesses or disorders. As a result, these issues or problems become subject to monitoring and control by medical professionals.

Doctors frequently appeared as expert witnesses at trial, effectively labelling some female defendants ill as opposed to criminal. Medical diagnoses therefore began to have legal implications, particularly within the field of psychiatry. There was widespread belief amongst the largely male medical establishment that women's female bodies made them prone to particular types of mania for example 'puerperal mania' (see box below) leading them to engage in criminal behaviour.

Key Term—Puerperal Mania

A condition occurring within two weeks of childbirth, characterised by restlessness, violence, obscene language, delusional state, refusal to eat and tendencies to fatally harm one's child. If puerperal mania continued past two weeks and symptoms became worse, it was then known as *puerperal insanity*. It was a complex mixture of myth and reality—during the 19th-century childbirth held many terrors both real and imagined.

Many women were committed to asylums following a diagnosis of puerperal insanity and this reinforced the insanity explanations for women's criminal behaviour particularly in terms of harming their own children. In addition, threads of religious doctrine were interwoven with medical discourse within the criminal justice system, particularly prominently in cases of infanticide. Although there was no official legal distinction between deaths of newborn babies and older children, in practice they were treated rather differently. This related to the timing of baptism—prior to baptism, children were not generally considered to have been accorded status as children, therefore those who died prior to their baptism were treated in the same way as if they had been stillborn. However, despite this, women who killed older children were rarely sentenced to death and were more likely to get life in prison, particularly given the strength of the victim narrative.

Not all women were affected equally by medicalisation—studies of the kleptomania defence amongst female shoplifters in the 19th-century have highlighted that whilst the crimes of respectable middle-class women were medicalised, working-class women were pathologised—so whilst middle-class female shoplifters came to be seen as "ill", working class women who shoplifted were "bad". In Mary Ann's case, there was little evidence of medicalisation. Her sanity did not appear to have been questioned to any significant degree—there is no mention of any type of "mania". Indeed she murdered all of her children months or years after the post-natal time frame and was not reported to have displayed any of the symptoms associated with this condition. Nor was she presented as suffering from the "weak and feeble mindedness" that was often associated with female crime. However, she was very much pathologised as she had deviated significantly from the nurturing ideal of motherhood applied to both working-class and middle-class women.

Women's crime in the 19th-century was increasingly medicalised, albeit selectively, often highlighting significant social class divisions in justice. Whilst Mary Ann's case was notable due to the *absence* of medical discourses at the time of her trial in 1873, a recent study by two authors of this book suggests that she may have had a personality disorder. Wilson and Yardley (2013) drew upon Hare's psychopathy checklist (revised) (PCL-R)—which we examined in *Chapter Two*—and applied this checklist to Mary Ann, so as to determine whether or not she would now be labelled as a psychopath, and if her behaviour can be solely accounted for in this way. The results in relation to each of the criteria and evidence in support of each score are provided in *Table 1*.

Table 1. Clinical examples and consensus scores for the 20 PCL-R items Mary Ann Cotton

Item	Score	Examples
1. Glibness/ superficial charm	2	Frequently and quickly established herself in different communities, making friends easily and gaining employment in a number of households. See Jane Hedley's account and note that she was "very friendly" with Cotton, even though Mary Ann had just moved into the village.

Item	Score	Examples
2. Grandiose sense of self-worth	2	Often employed women to clean for her and predicted the deaths of her mother and her step son. She was happy to challenge the medical competency of doctors.
3. Proneness to boredom / need for stimulation	0	There is no documentary evidence to support this.
4. Pathological lying	2	She was happy to pretend that the ailments of her family members were not the result of arsenic poisoning; she maintained her innocence in the face of overwhelming evidence to the contrary.
5. Conning / manipulative	2	She had a history of multiple, concurrent relationships — note that she established a relationship with Quick-Manning almost as soon as she started to nurse him, all the while maintaining a relationship with a man named Joseph Nattrass. She fraudulently withdrew the money of James Robinson.
6. Lack of remorse or guilt	2	She maintained her innocence until her execution, and while the fact that she was on a capital charge may have affected her ability to show remorse/guilt there is nothing in the public record to imply that she cared about what had happened to her victims.
7. Shallow affect	1	During interviews she was mostly dramatic, e.g. demanding to see James Robinson and the child that she abandoned with a friend.
8. Callousness / lack of empathy	2	Evidenced by her crimes.
9. Parasitic lifestyle	1	She worked as a housekeeper and this seems to have given her access to men (and others) that she could then use to her own ends. However, she also worked as a dressmaker and as a nurse.

Item	Score	Examples
10. Poor behavioural controls	0	There is no documentary evidence to support this within the historical record, although choosing to abandon Robinson when she appeared to have achieved a comfortable lifestyle is perhaps suggestive of poor behavioural control.
11. Promiscuous sexual behaviour	2	She used her ability to establish relationships with men as a means to gain access to them and their households. There was some reporting after her execution that she was a "'prostitute". She probably killed her stepson Charles because she had established a new relationship with Quick-Manning in West Auckland.
12. Early behaviour problems	0	There is no evidence to support this in the historical record.
13. Lack of realistic long term goals	2	She lived a somewhat nomadic, day-to-day existence, and her abandoning of her baby in Sunderland—which she then demanded to see when she was in Durham Gaol—indicates that she had no clear view of what she actually wanted.
14. Impulsivity	2	There are numerous examples of poor impulse control in her adult life.
15. Irresponsibility	0	This item does not seem to apply—in fact she wanted responsibility, as evidenced by the fact that she became first a Sunday School teacher and then a nurse.
16. Failure to accept responsibility for own actions	2	She maintained her innocence throughout her trial and brief imprisonment.
17. Many short term marital relationships	2	Based on the definition of "marriage" as any live-in relationship that involved some degree of commitment she had at least four "marriages".
18. Juvenile delinquency	0	No evidence of this in the historical record.

Item	Score	Examples
19. Revocation of conditional release	0	No evidence of this in the historical record.
20. Criminal versatility	1	Fraud in relation to James Robinson.

Adapted from Wilson and Yardley, 2013, p. 25

These results suggest that Mary Ann was a psychopath—at least in the British context—as her total score is 25. However, is this micro-analysis an adequate explanation of her behaviour? In short, is it enough to simply look at her personality and character to understand the murders that she committed, and to be satisfied to explain these by labelling her as a "psychopath"? Surely the answers for what motivated Cotton to commit her crimes have to also be based on broader structural issues too? This is an important question, which we address in the following section.

Institutional Understandings of Mary Ann Cotton

In *Chapter Seven*, we introduced the 'institutional' approach to understanding female serial killers, emphasising the potential value of exploring structures such as the polity (or political system), economy, education, family and religion; bodies like schools, businesses, charities and faith-based organisations; and roles including mother, father, worker, student, volunteer. In applying the institutional approach to Mary Ann's case, we demonstrate how 19th-century institutions shaped and influenced the social world she inhabited and explore her dynamic relationship with those institutions. The material we drew upon in doing this included 19th-century newspaper accounts about the case, Mary Ann's surviving letters, and public records held about her at the National Archives such as the evidence given at her trial. We identified the nature of Mary Ann's engagement with institutional frames of reference—or in other words how she participated in social life as a member of society. We did this through looking carefully at her social positions and roles, focusing upon the three parts of institutions: structure; regulation; and performance. We posed the following questions in relation to each one:

- *Structure*: What were Cotton's individual circumstances? What was the wider social context in which she committed her crimes? What were the "rules"? How *should* she have been behaving, what were the *expectations* for someone in her position?
- *Regulation*: To what extent did Cotton conform to the rules? To what extent did the usual rewards or punishments affect her behaviour?
- *Performance*: What did she achieve or lose by adhering to or breaking the rules? In what way did she benefit from killing?
- We present our summarised findings in *Table 2* below and then expand upon them in relation to each social role.

Social Identities	Institution(s)	Institutional Component		
		Structure	Regulation	Performance
Wife	Family Economy Religion Polity	• Marriage, widowhood / remarriage; • Dependency; • Husband's work; • Respectable women; • Clean home.	• Excessive and rapid remarriages; • Exceeded what was "normal"; • Geographical mobility; • Respectable veneer; • Employed cleaners.	• Was seen as a "respectable" woman until later years; • However, she destroyed multiple manifestations of the family.
Mother	Family	• Cherish and care for children; • Parental responsibility — prioritisation of child's needs over own; • Acceptable discipline; • Acceptable infanticide.	• Appeared to be a good mother at times; • Own needs first; • Overstepped discipline boundaries; • Unacceptable murder.	• Excessive mortality of her children.
Worker	Economy Family	• Working class women engage in paid labour; • Little recognition for labour; • Supplement husband's income; • Home workers — landlady, seamstress, (prostitute).	• Nurse; • Servant; • Children — barrier to paid labour; • Landlady — numerous households.	• Generated income from paid labour; • Income from lodgers; • Surveillance of lodgers — damage limitation.

Social Identities	Institution(s)	Institutional Component		
		Structure	Regulation	Performance
Christian	Religion Polity	• Wesleyan Methodist Church; • Responsibility through confession; • Repentance.	• Part-time Wesleyan; • Never confesses to murder and blames others for acquisitive crimes; • Presentation of religion as a protective mechanism.	• Re-engagement with religion fails to secure a reprieve; • Matthew Hall sees through her act.
Fraudster / Thief	Family Economy	• Acquisitive crime — sometimes necessary; • Victims — extra-familial; • Getting caught — consequences.	• Did not need to commit acquisitive crime; • Victims — familial and employer; • Getting away with it.	• Acquisitive crime — power not greed; • Defrauding men rather than depending upon them.
Murderer	Family Polity	• Tolerance of infanticide; • Female murderers — mad/bad/insane/evil; • Burial insurance.	• Not infanticide — systematic and planned murders; • Social construction of a monster; • Husbands and children insured.	• Insurance payouts; • Murder as emancipation or homicidal protest.

Table 2: The Institutional Context of Mary Ann Cotton

Wife

Marriage was essential for women in the 19th-century North-East, who were dependent upon their husbands for survival. It was however difficult to get out of and divorce was an expensive option beyond the reach of many working-class women. Many women were widowed though—their husbands the victims of the hazardous work in the mining industry and poor health in these communities—therefore remarriage was common and acceptable. Family life revolved around the husband's work and would often dictate where the family lived. In relation to Mary Ann, whilst remarriage was normal, the number of times she remarried was out of the ordinary. Furthermore, she got married in secret a few times— away from the eyes of friends and relatives—and she did not conduct all of these relationships in front of the same audience so this did not set alarm bells ringing for some time—she moved around from village to village under the auspices of her husband's job.

The idea of the "respectable woman" was a benchmark by which the behaviour of wives was judged, they should not have sexual relationships with men who were not their husbands and they were expected to keep their homes clean and tidy using the tools of the time—soft soap and arsenic. These expectations clearly had an impact upon how Mary Ann conducted herself as she had a respectable veneer—she was always married when she gave birth to her children (but she was always pregnant at the time of the wedding—aside from that to George Ward). She did indeed have a clean home, but she wasn't too keen on cleaning it herself—she employed cleaners to do it for her! And these cleaners would also be the ones sent out to the shop to buy arsenic and soft soap.

So in summary, what have we gleaned from examining Mary Ann's role as a wife? She did obtain the socially acceptable and expected outcomes of being married—marriage brought with it respectability and a degree of financial security (George Ward being the exception to this as his illness meant he was unable to work). So why did she not just settle down with William Mowbray, her first husband? Why did she systematically destroy or try to destroy every husband she had? Perhaps she was not satisfied with the mainstream outcomes of marriage. So what was she looking for? Let's have a look at her other social roles for some clues.

Mother

Much like today, mothers in the 19th-century North-East were expected to cherish and care for their children, putting children's needs before their own and taking responsibility for them. Victorian society did however believe that children's behaviour should be kept in line—so some discipline was necessary within defined boundaries. Mary Ann performed the role of the good mother to her audiences in the local community, particularly those who depended upon her for an income. At her trial, her cleaners described how she was kindly disposed to her children, and how she wept bitterly and took ill herself when they died. However, examining other evidence, she clearly put her own needs before those of her children—trying to offload Charles Edward when he became an inconvenience.

She also overstepped the discipline boundaries, in the later stage of her murderous career neighbours who saw her beating Charles Edward commented that she was using excessive force, Mary Ann's neighbour Margaret Priestley suggested that she had taken discipline too far,

> ...she struck him against the wall with her hand. His head came against the wall. She took her foot up and bunched him...I could see that she often left him at eight o'clock in the morning, and didn't came back till late at night. She would lock him outside...I have five children, and I beat them in a right manner. I have what I call a belt in my house—it has no buckle on. I use it single. I never take my foot or knee to them...The strap was one belonging to the lodger, with a buckle, such as pitmen wear. (Durham Spring Assizes—Wednesday, 1873, p. 3)

As discussed earlier in the chapter, killing a child was socially—if not legally—acceptable in tightly defined circumstances, notably when another mouth to feed would plunge the family further into poverty. In relation to Mary Ann, the children she killed were not new-borns and she was not in grinding poverty at the time of their deaths. In terms of what we can learn from looking at Mary Ann's role as a mother, given harsh social conditions it would have been expected that *some* of her children might die—but *most* of her children did. Rather than having healthy, happy, appropriately disciplined children, Mary Ann selfishly pursued her own ends. She exercised the ultimate power in disposing of the inconvenient children she resented as the trapdoors that compelled her into marriage and were the unfortunate side effect of performance of the good wife role

Worker

It was usual for working-class women in the 19th-century North-East to engage in paid labour outside the home (in direct contrast to middle-class women—for whom this was perceived as very odd indeed). However, their work would receive very little recognition—Mary Ann's marriage certificate to George Ward did not even state her occupation, she was a nurse at the time. Rates of pay were low and far from sufficient to sustain them as single women. Therefore a woman's paid labour would simply *supplement* her husband's income. It was also usual for women to work within the home—taking in lodgers, doing work such as sewing and in some circumstances prostitution, which was frowned upon but was generally tolerated if women were not married—widows were included in this category.

In relation to Mary Ann's work, she was considered to be a good nurse—employers at Sunderland Infirmary spoke highly of her and they were among the few people who lodged a petition for the commutation of her death sentence. However, she also worked as a servant for a doctor in the time after leaving James Robinson—and certainly bent some of the rules here. We know she was not keen on cleaning her own home but this extended to the home she was employed to clean in her job as a servant too. She sub-contracted the cleaning work out to other women—paying them with items she had stolen from the doctor. Considering all this, we can see that Mary Ann was able to bring additional income into the home when she was married—but she also seemed to survive well when she was not married—she got what she needed. Her children didn't though—they were described as pale and skinny and generally quite sickly. In her time as a widow she frequently complained that the children were a barrier to her engaging in paid labour but she did take in lodgers during this time so was not without an income. However, there was one unintended consequence of having lodgers—in being a permanent fixture in her home, they became an informal type of surveillance—they could see what she was doing day in, day out.

One lodger—Joseph Nattrass—proved particularly problematic—he had known Mary Ann for several years and was reported to have had a sexual relationship with her. It could be argued that he had worked out what she was doing given this quote from a newspaper report of the trial:

> "The poor fellow obviously suspected that all was not right, for, on being visited by one of his companions, he remarked, 'If I was only better, I would be out of this'. The day before his death, he told his medical attendant, Dr Richardson, who had been treating him for gastric fever, that he had no more fever than he (the doctor) had, and if it was not for that grinding pain in his stomach, he was all right, and he actually refused to take any more of the doctors medicine shortly before his death, which occurred on April last." (*Northern Echo*, 1873, p. 3)

Another lodger of Mary Ann's—a man by the name of Lowrey—urged her to confess her sins in his letters to her in prison, suggesting that he too had some knowledge of her extraordinary activities.

Christian

The Methodist Wesleyan Church was thriving in North-East England during the 19th-century. Important principles that guided the lives of its members were taking responsibility, being truthful and confessing your sins—being repentant when you had sinned. Mary Ann was what we might call a "part time" Wesleyan—she appears to have abandoned the church in her early twenties only to re-engage with it when she thought it would help her cause for a commutation. She never confessed to murdering Charles Edward or any of the others and with reference to her theft and fraud—for which there was undisputable evidence—she simply said that she was driven to it and it wasn't her fault.

Mary Ann may have expected that re-engaging with the church would lead to widespread sympathy for her amongst fellow Christians and a subsequent reprieve would be granted. It didn't quite work out this way. In fact, some people saw straight through this altogether. We see evidence of this in a letter sent to Mary Ann from an old childhood friend—Matthew Hall, who had seen letters she had exchanged with another childhood contemporary, Henry Holdforth,

> I have just read your letter to Holdforth, in the Daily Paper and you appear to have cast your thoughts back on your former days, when a Sabbath School Teacher, when your Dear Mother was also a member of the Wesleyan Society, these were Happy days—and you know it—you had a good Mother and a good bringing up. You were taught the Principles of the Religion of the Bible and now where are you?
>
> You seem to have a Hope of Heaven—be sure that Hope is well founded. A mere formal notion or wish, will avail you nothing, you must seek it earnestly with your whole heart, and with Tears—let not a moment slip…I write in the presence of God to take heed and let not your Soul be Lost through negligence or delay—but make immediate Effort and seek the Saviour. (Letter to Mary Ann Cotton from Matthew Hall, 21st March 1873, reprinted in Appleton (1973, p. 124))

Fraudster / Thief

Looking back at 19th-century England, we see particular understandings of acquisitive crime developing. Many believed that it was a function of the emerging capitalist society—people wanted to join in and have the goods that were being produced by the industries around them—they were becoming *consumers.* However, they needed money to buy such items—and if they couldn't obtain these things legitimately, some might steal them from other people. On the whole, people tended not to steal from their own families because if they were poor it was likely their family was poor as well. But when people did engage in property crime, they would get caught eventually.

Mary Ann was an acquisitive criminal—she defrauded her husband James Robinson—stealing money that she was supposed to be depositing in his bank account. She also stole from her employer—the doctor for whom she worked as a servant. But what doesn't seem to fit with the social norms in relation to her acquisitive crime is that she didn't *need* to do it—she was married to James Robinson at the time—a relatively wealthy man. In addition, the items she stole from the doctor were used as payment for her sub-contractors—she didn't keep these things for herself. But perhaps the most interesting thing is that Mary Ann got away with her acquisitive crimes, she took flight when Robinson found out she had stolen his money so there were no criminal justice consequences in relation to this crime and when her employer discovered her thefts he simply gave her a stern talking to. Therefore as an acquisitive criminal, Mary Ann was quite unlike other acquisitive criminals of her era—but maybe her crimes were not about greed or consumption. Maybe this was about power. This is particularly the case in relation to James Robinson—by taking his money she was gaining back some control. In stealing from him she was challenging the norm of women's dependency upon their husbands.

Murderer

So what about Mary Ann's performance in the role we know her best—that of a murderer? We know from earlier that infanticide amongst the impoverished was tolerated to a degree but that Mary Ann's crimes exceeded the tightly defined boundaries around this. Mary Ann's murders were clearly not infanticide—her children were older and she killed her husbands and other adults in addition. In terms of women who killed outside of this frame of reference, 19th-century England understood them as mad or bad, insane or evil monsters, their crimes part of a psychosis or a demonic rage who weren't in control of their actions.

However, Mary Ann's murders were systematic, carefully planned and concealed—this is not particularly consistent with someone not in control of their actions. In addition, Mary Ann was reported to have been an attractive woman, so it was difficult to construct her as a monster or aberration—even though the press tried to do so, as we noted earlier, her pictures were altered to make her appear more "scary".

Society did however find another way of making sense of her murders. There were growing concerns around the abuse of "burial insurance" in the late 19th-century—policies taken out by parents that would result in a cash payment if their child died. It was thought that some unscrupulous parents might kill their children simply to obtain the money from the policies. Mary Ann insured all of her husbands and children—aside from James Robinson who refused to sign the paperwork—and indeed, received insurance payouts upon their deaths. As such, the Victorians understood her murders as financially motivated—she was very much the *Black Widow* with elements of *For Profit* if we apply the typology of Kelleher and Kelleher (1998). If it was the burial insurance that motivated her, then she succeeded for a while as she was able to obtain several payouts. However, these were not large amounts of money—the government had placed limits on how much children could be insured for—she could by no means "retire" on these sums and as we saw in her role as a *Worker*, she was very much able to support herself by less risky means—suggesting that the Victorian understanding of her murders as financially motivated is not sufficient.

Mary Ann Cotton the Emancipatory Murderer?

As we have seen, Mary Ann was able to get away with murder for years, systematically creating and destroying the manifestations of the family that she created. Perhaps it was this destruction itself that is the key to making sense of her actions? We suggest that it is worth considering her murders as more or less emancipatory efforts—albeit dysfunctional and antisocial ones—to break gender norms and perform a personal protest against the one institution that constrained her—the family. It is here that Kelleher and Kelleher's *Revenge* killer may enter the frame—albeit with a richer contextual rooting.

The family in North-East 19th-century England was one in which women were "defined by, and defined themselves by, their home and family… mining women were baby-makers and drudges, doubly oppressed by capitalism and by their husbands" (Hall, 2004, pp. 522–525). Mary Ann was living in a society where her life was largely confined to the family and the roles of wife and mother within this institution. In terms of getting away with murder, social identities which were incompatible with the wife and the mother simply went unseen. The gender power imbalance of 19th-century Victorian England would appear to have enabled rather than constrained Mary Ann's behaviour. She did indeed enjoy a dynamic relationship with the institutions that formed the backdrop to her life—she successfully performed socially acceptable behaviour within the different institutions drawing upon mainstream norms and values. She did this very convincingly in some instances –and when these acts began to wear thin she was able to draw upon the norm of geographical mobility to start afresh.

Mary Ann was able to continue this working and reworking of the institutional templates up until the point where she began to present conflicting social identities to her audience in the form of Thomas Riley. Presented with Mary Ann the versatile criminal and Mary Ann the bad mother, he began to scrutinise this woman's behaviour more closely before activating a formal channel of regulation—the local police sergeant—as a check on her behaviour—an act which ultimately led to the end of a long and tragic career as a poisoner.

Given what we have discovered about the dominance of the family in Mary Ann's life, we can suggest that her serial murders were a response to her constrained position in the institutional landscape. She did not withdraw her commitment to the family, in fact, she continuously re-engaged with this institution. Abandoning the family was simply not an option—19th-century North-East England was not a place where single women could support themselves (Wilson, 2013). Therefore, Mary Ann needed the family for her survival, and unlike her dissatisfied contemporaries, she did not simply tolerate the constraints and gender inequality that participation in this institution entailed. Survival was intertwined with the social identities of wife and mother and could not be disentangled from the family. Continually starting over with new manifestations of the family was perhaps Mary Ann's way of exercising the ultimate power over an institution in which women were traditionally powerless.

Revision

- How many people is Mary Ann Cotton believed to have killed?
- What was her relationship to these victims?
- Is there any one "type" of female serial killer that easily explains Mary Ann Cotton's motivations? If so, why? If not, why not?
- What does an "institutional" approach bring to the study of serial murder?
- What factors are examined when an "institutional" approach is taken?

Further Reading

For those interested in exploring the case of Mary Ann Cotton in more detail, we would recommend D Wilson (2013), *Mary Ann*

Cotton: Britain's First Female Serial Killer, Winchester: Waterside Press. Arthur Appleton (1973), *Mary Ann Cotton*, London: Michael Joseph is also a useful introduction to the case but is now out of print and copies are consequently difficult to come by.

SERIAL KILLERS AND THE MEDIA

9

"[Serial killers] capture attention by capitalizing on deeply resonate themes of innocent victims, dangerous strangers, unsolved murders, all coalescing around a narrative of evasion and given moral force through implied personal threats to audience members. Serial killers were apparently ready-made for prime time."

(Kevin Haggerty, 2009).

This final chapter is concerned with the media's relationship with and their portrayal of serial killers and the phenomenon of serial murder. This is an issue which we have touched on in previous chapters and especially when we considered the case of Joanne Dennehy. What was it about (wrongly) applying the label of "serial killer" to her and "serial murder" to her crimes that made her, and others like her, in the words of the Canadian academic Kevin Haggerty, "ready-made for prime time"? Haggerty has gone further and has even suggested that "serial killing is patterned in modernity's self-image" and that, as a result, modernity provides "the key institutional frameworks, motivations, and opportunity structures characteristic of contemporary forms of serial killing" (Haggerty, 2009: 170).

One of the key institutional frameworks to which Haggerty draws attention is the rise of the mass media, and while there have always been scholars who have been interested in how serial killers are presented in the media, Haggerty suggests that "a symbiotic relationship exists between the media and serial killers. In the quest for audience share the media have become addicted to portrayals of serial killers",

(Haggerty, 2009: 174). Haggerty's ideas will form the academic context for the arguments being made within the rest of the chapter.

Of course, the whole territory of the media's use of crime—especially violent crime—is a very broad, well-researched issue that many academics have written about previously and the issue itself has a long history (and see below). Usually this academic interest can be seen as having three different strands: does the media portrayal of crime have an effect on actual crime; how crime news stereotypes some groups, which might lead to a "moral panic"; and, finally, how crime and punishment are represented and then consumed by their various audiences.

At first glance these three different strands do not seem to have much relevance to our study of serial murder and serial killers. However, in relation to "media effects", we might note the case of Canadian Mark Twitchell, the so-called "Dexter Killer", who was charged and convicted in 2011 for the murder of John Altinger. Twitchell—an aspiring filmmaker who shot a horror movie in 2008—claimed to have been inspired to commit murder by the TV series *Dexter* (2006–2013) which was, in turn, based on the novels of Jeff Lindsay, about Dexter Morgan, a serial killer who nonetheless worked as a blood spatter analyst for the police. Closer to home is the case of Stephen Griffiths, who murdered three sex workers in Bradford between 2009 and 2010. Griffiths, who was studying for a PhD at the University of Bradford in homicide studies, originally gave his name at Bradford Magistrate's Court as "The Crossbow Cannibal", fully aware that this would create the headlines that he wanted to generate about himself. It is also clear that he used his academic knowledge about serial murder within the murders that he committed and was reviewing various books about serial murder on Amazon. We might also note the case of Colin Ireland, the so-called "Gay Slayer", who murdered five men between March and June 1993 in London. Ireland claimed that he had killed these men because he wanted to become famous and, after reading FBI profiler Robert Ressler's (1992) *Whoever Fights Monsters*, decided that he could achieve that objective through becoming a serial killer.

So too, we have previously suggested in *Chapter One*, that the FBI used serial murder to create a moral panic about what they claimed was a new and unprecedented phenomenon and which had, in the words of Ressler, reached "epidemic proportions", to lobby for the creation of the National Center for the Analysis of Violent Crime (NCAVC). It was only later that more reasoned analyses suggested that the numbers of murders committed each year by serial killers was 50 to 60 in the United States, rather than the 4,000 claimed by the FBI. By then the NCAVC had already been established.

In thinking about how offenders are represented and how crime might be consumed by an audience we have also suggested that the media's use of crime and criminals started a long time ago. For example, we can trace the detective novel to Edgar Allan Poe's 1841 short story *The Murder in the Rue Morgue,* which also undoubtedly influenced Conan Doyle's work, especially his novels involving the character Sherlock Holmes. Holmes first appeared in 1887—the year before Jack the Ripper. So too autobiographies of serving or former prisoners, which are a staple of the "true crime" genre, can trace their origins back to the picaresque novels of the 18th-century, the exemplary confessions contained within the *Newgate Calendar* and even execution broadsheet pamphlets which were distributed on "hanging days".

In relation to serial killers, there are also a small number of autobiographies, such as Carl Panzram (1970), *Panzram: A Journal of Murder* (Panzram murdered at least 21 people in the USA), and Ian Brady's (2001) *The Gates of Janus: Serial Killing and Its Analysis.* This latter, wholly self-serving book, is not technically an autobiography, but it is the closest that Brady has come to outlining why he committed murder, although he usually discusses other serial killers and their motives. Perhaps the best example of a true crime account which also allows us to glimpse the reality behind the murders that the killer committed remains Brian Masters (1985) *Killing for Company,* about the serial killer Dennis Nilsen. This best-selling book undoubtedly benefits from the fact that Masters gained access to Nilsen's writings and interviewed him and members of his family at length.

As these examples also suggest, when we use the word "media"—or, as it is sometimes described more popularly, the "mass media"—we are employing a shorthand to describe a number of different commodities, industries and their products. These products can include, at the very least, novels, true crime accounts, newspapers, magazines, blogs, films, computer games, TV programmes and documentaries, with various print and broadcast journalists, and film and TV producers—all working within these industries with their own different histories and commercial pressures—often vying with each other to sell more tickets or newspapers, or to generate a bigger audience for their product. In short, we need to remember that the word "media" is a description that masks a variety of different "medias".

We are concerned in this chapter with newspapers, and news coverage on television about "real" serial killers, rather than with fictional serial killers such as Dexter, Hannibal Lector, or series such as *The Following* or *The Fall*. However, what is also interesting—but beyond the scope of this chapter—is how fiction and reality might become confused by the audience, so that the boundary between what is real and what is imagined becomes eroded with the growing popularity or infamy of some characters who are portrayed within the mass media. This is sometimes called "mediatisation".

Key Term — Mediatisation

Mediatisation is a term employed within post-modern theory to describe how the media complicates the division between reality and media representations of reality and so helps to erode the division between fact and fiction.

Given the breadth and complexity of all of this background and history, we will structure the chapter around just a few questions which should help us to get to an answer as to why and how the print and broadcast news media portrays serial killers and the phenomenon of serial murder. These questions relate to trying to understand just why the media are so obsessed with violent crime through a consideration of what are known as "news values", or more broadly, "newsworthiness" and then becoming more critical about all of this by discussing *which* serial killers become "prime time" and those who disappear from public view.

The idea of serial killers disappearing from public view might appear like an odd observation to make. However, as we will show, there are some serial killers who are "prime time", whilst others barely register on public consciousness. Have you heard of, for example, Trevor Hardy (whom we consider in detail below), Peter Moore, or Robin Ligus? Moore is a Welsh serial killer who murdered four men in North Wales between September and December 1995, and was a well-known local businessman who owned a chain of cinemas. Ligus—from Shrewsbury—was convicted of murdering Robert Young during a burglary in 1994, but in 2010 was charged with three further murders which had also been committed in Shropshire in 1994. He was later found guilty of two of these murders—those of Trevor Bradley and Brian Coles. As such, both Moore and Ligus[1] are "serial killers" by the definition which we use within this book but, we suggest, are not very well-known to the public.

Crime and the News

There have been generations of criminologists who have looked more generally at crime reporting, and while crime—like sex—has been a subject of popular fascination long before the rise of the mass media, there is little doubt that crime is a major feature of the contemporary news agenda. It is also clear that the media do not publish or broadcast every criminal act that is within the public domain, but are selective of the kinds of crimes, criminals and circumstances upon which they report. Some criminal acts are chosen over others because of their "newsworthiness". In other words, those aspects of a crime that print and broadcast journalists argue make for a good news story, a judgment which is, in turn, a product of the newsroom

1. There remain doubts as to Ligus's guilt and so we do not include him within our list of serial killers.

culture of their industries. As a result it is also widely accepted that the most commonly reported crimes—which would include serial killing—are those that happen less frequently. The criminologist Robert Reiner, for example, has demonstrated in his study of British newspapers from 1945 that homicide was by far the most common type of crime reported, accounting for about one-third of all crime news stories throughout the period. More popularly this selection of news stories is sometimes called "If it bleeds, it leads", and remember too that "news" is simply the plural of "new".

Based on early attempts to categorise news values and the influential work of Steve Chibnall (1977), Yvonne Jewkes has expanded further on this notion of "newsworthiness" and has suggested a 12-point criteria of "news values for a new millennium" (Jewkes, 2004: 40–55). These news values, she argues, become the bases for the judgment that print and broadcast journalists and editors will make in gauging the level of public interest that a story will generate. Jewkes's news values include:

(i) *Threshold*: Asking whether a story is significant enough to be of interest to a national audience;

(ii) *Predictability*: Vital resources are often committed to pre-planned events ensuring their place on the running-order;

(iii) *Simplification*: A crime story must be "reducible to a minimum number of parts or themes";

(iv) *Individualism*: Stories must have a "human interest" appeal and be easy to relate to;

(v) *Risk*: We could all be victims with little attention given to crime avoidance;

(vi) *Sex*: Sexual violence, "stranger-danger" and female offenders being portrayed as sexual predators;

(vii) *Celebrity or high status persons*: The media is attracted to all elements of celebrity and crime is no different;

(viii) *Proximity*: Both spatially and culturally;

(ix) *Violence*: As with sex, it fulfils the media's desire for drama;

(x) *Spectacle and graphic imagery*: Particularly for television news;

(xi) *Children*: Either as victims or offenders;

(xii) *Conservative ideology and political diversion*: Protecting the "British way of life'".

We can see, for example, several of these news values in operation with Joanne Dennehy, all of which allowed her and her crimes to become "prime time". Most immediately her murders involved sex and violence; there was graphic imagery with pictures of Dennehy posing with a large knife, and she also had a distinctive, star tattoo on her cheek; and, of course, she was also a female offender, who could be portrayed as a sexual predator or, more academically, as "doubly deviant".

Key Term — Doubly Deviant

The idea of women being doubly deviant helps to explain the media's interest in their crimes and the greater public vilification that they receive. Not only have they broken the law, but they are also seen to have deviated from "natural" roles that women should occupy, such as being a mother, wife, care-giver.

We can also see in the Dennehy case threshold, simplification, risk, individualism and predictability. In relation to the first and last of these news values, for example, someone who had killed three men and had attempted to kill two others, was always going to meet the threshold that would prompt a news story to have national, as opposed to simply local or regional significance. So too, given that the media knew when and where her case was coming to trial, arrangements could be made to have journalists at court to report on the conduct of the trial, which in turn allowed newspaper editors, or TV and radio producers to determine what would be covered within the news on the days that the trial lasted. In other words, there was predictability to the story, which also helped to ensure that the resources needed to report on the story—such as journalists, camera crews and so forth—were suitably allocated.

However, if all of this is accurate—and we would suggest that by and large it is—why do some cases of serial murder gain prominence, whilst others disappear from public view? Is Beverly Allitt, for example, just as infamous as Rose West or Myra Hindley? Why is Peter Dinsdale, who killed 26 people in the early-1980s, relatively unknown, while there can be few people who will not have heard of Peter Sutcliffe—who was known in the media as the "Yorkshire Ripper"? Let's consider this question further by discussing the case of the serial killer Trevor Hardy. Why has his case "disappeared" from public and academic scrutiny? Why was his case not "newsworthy" and what might this lack of attention suggest about Jewkes's news values. In doing so what we seek to do is to examine why some serial killers emerge into popular and academic consciousness while others disappear, and thus to re-consider how "newsworthiness" and the symbiotic relationship between the serial killer and the media coexist.

However, given that the Hardy case is so little-known, we start by describing this more fully and provide some background—largely culled from local newspaper accounts, or from the co-written autobiography of Geoffrey Garrett (Garrett and Nott, 2001), the Home Office pathologist who worked on the case—about the murders that Hardy committed.

Trevor Joseph Hardy

Trevor Joseph Hardy was born on 11 June in 1945 in Manchester, England. He was 31-years-old when he was sentenced to life for three counts of murder on 2 May 1977 and, until his death in HMP Wakefield in 2013, was one of Britain's longest serving prisoners. His criminal career began when he was just eight-years-old. At the age of 15 years he was sent to the adult prison, HMP Strangeways, for burglary—the judge telling him that despite his young age he would be jailed "for the public's protection". In 1963 Hardy was sentenced to one month in prison for indecent exposure, and Garrett and Nott describe Hardy as having an exterior "hard-as-nails" spirit, despite his slim 5ft 7in build. However, they say that in private he was "unusually close to his mother" having few "normal relationships with girlfriends", and that he "enjoyed dressing up in women's clothes" (Garrett and Nott, 2001: 135).

Reports from the *Manchester Evening News* (1975–7) build up a picture of Hardy's dysfunctional love life. In his early twenties he entered into a platonic relationship with an older woman, then after leaving prison at the age of 27 years he became besotted with a 15-year-old schoolgirl named Beverley Driver. Hardy almost immediately ended up in prison again, this time for assaulting a man named Stanley O'Brien with a pickaxe during a row over a round of drinks. Hardy claimed he had been set up, and vowed to kill O'Brien. He also wanted to kill Beverley Driver, because she had, by then, ended contact with him at her parents' request.

On his release from prison Hardy discovered that O'Brien had already died, and all his anger was vented towards Beverley. On New Year's Eve 1974, just a month after having been released from prison on parole, he claimed his first victim—15-year-old Janet Stewart—whom he mistook for Beverley. According to court records Janet had been walking to meet her boyfriend in a public house on New Year's Eve 1974, but she failed to turn up. It was not until Hardy confessed to her murder on 27 August 1975 that her family finally knew what had happened to her. In the presence of his solicitor, Hardy told police that he had seen Janet getting out of a car at around 10.40pm and, mistaking her for his former girlfriend, he stabbed her in the throat, cut her neck and then dragged her body into a hollow and covered her. In March 1975 he returned to the shallow grave to bury her properly. Hardy then returned to the grave once more to remove her head, hands and feet, either to conceal her identity, or as "some very strange form of gratification" (Garrett and Nott, 2001: 138). It later emerged that Hardy had, in fact, returned to the body to steal Janet's ring to give to his new girlfriend—Sheilagh Farrow—a divorcee ten years his senior. On 1 September 1976 he revisited the scene with his solicitor and showed police the waste ground where he had disposed of Janet's body. He later boasted in court that school children had seen him at the grave.

Hardy's second victim was a barmaid called Wanda Skala. She was 18-years-old when Hardy murdered her in the early hours of the morning on 19 July 1975. Wanda had been working at the Lightbowne Hotel in Moston, Manchester the previous evening and, after closing time, stayed on for a drink with some friends and some of the staff. Bill Stewart—the father of Hardy's first victim Lesley, also worked at the hotel and may even have served his daughter's killer. Wanda left at around 2.15 a.m. At 10.00 a.m. her body was found on a nearby building site, although she had been partially buried. The clothes on the upper part of her body had been torn open, her right breast had been bitten, and her trousers and underwear had been almost entirely removed. Her right sock had been tied around her neck. A post mortem examination revealed her cause of death to be severe head injures and strangulation and that:

> "The head injuries were consistent with having been caused by a large number of heavy blows possibly from a brick found at the scene. Part of the right nipple had been removed, possibly by biting and there was a lacerated wound and bruising near the upper part of the vulva which could have been caused by kicking or a blow from a blunt object." (Teare, 2008)

In a police statement, Hardy said that he had read about a killer named Neville Heath in a book from Queen's Park Library, and had made the scene look like a sex attack. Heath—who bit off a nipple from one of his victims—was hanged in 1946 for the murders of two women, although police suspected that he had killed a third.

Hardy was immediately a suspect, but when the police visited his flat in Smedley Road, Newton Heath, Manchester, Farrow provided him with an alibi, and had already washed the blood from his clothes. She later told the jury that Hardy had confessed to killing Janet and had shown her where he had buried the body. It was also to emerge that she had helped Hardy hide behind an old fireplace in their flat when the police arrived. In the autumn of 1975 Hardy's brother, Colin, told police that his brother had confessed to the murder of Wanda while they were out drinking together and, as a result, Hardy was taken in for questioning. Displaying some forensic awareness, Hardy realised that he had left clues on Wanda's body, and so asked Farrow to smuggle in a file in order to rasp his teeth down so as to prevent the police linking him to the bite marks on his victim. The lack of dental evidence—and the fact that Farrow had given him an alibi—forced the police to release Hardy which allowed him to kill again.

As with Hardy's previous victims, Sharon Mosoph was a young woman who was just 17-years-old when she died on 9 March 1976. Sharon—whose small stature earned her the nickname of "Titch"—had arrived in Manchester the previous evening and she had walked to the night bus stop with a friend. Some time later, screams were heard from the direction of the Rochdale Canal. At around 8.00 a.m. on 9 March 1976 her naked body was found. Sharon's tights had been used to strangle her. When the frozen canal melted, a bundle of her clothes and her handbag came to the surface. Detectives believed she had been attacked whilst walking along the street, then dragged on her back across a car park, and thrown into the canal. Again, one of her nipples was missing. Police suggested that Sharon may have confronted Hardy as he was trying to break into Marlborough Mill, where she worked as a cashier.

Once more Hardy realised that he may have left clues on his victim's body, so he returned to the scene. He found Sharon's body in the canal and mutilated it, erasing his teeth marks from her nipple. Hardy then appears to have left the area and, while living rough, he sexually and physically assaulted another woman in a public toilet. On 29 June 1976 Hardy appeared at Oldham Magistrates' Court charged with the murders of Sharon Mosoph and Wanda Skala, amid chaotic scenes from the victims' families. There was a second hearing on 6 July when Hardy's mother protested her son's innocence. He was driven from court to the screams of "monster" and "murdering bastard".

After the police charged Hardy with the murders of Wanda and Sharon he confessed to killing Lesley, who had, up until then, still been treated as a missing person. Despite his confession, Hardy pleaded not guilty to murder at his trial at Manchester Crown Court. Instead, he pleaded guilty to manslaughter on the grounds of diminished responsibility. On the fourth day of the trial, when Farrow was due to give evidence against him, Hardy sacked his counsel and began to conduct his own defence. The jury didn't believe him and convicted him of the three counts of murder having retired for just 70 minutes. He was sentenced to life imprisonment. During sentencing the judge, Mr Justice Caulfield, described Hardy as "hopelessly evil" and praised the police for their hard work.

Sharon's father, Ralph, attempted to pursue Farrow in the civil courts, but due to the £15,000 needed for a private prosecution he was forced to give up. However, in 1981 he received a letter from Hardy who was in HM Prison Hull, spelling out further details about the murders. An enquiry was launched, but the Prison Service concluded that the letter was smuggled out with the help of a relative. On 16 December 1994, the then Home Secretary, Michael Howard, set the period to be served by Hardy, to satisfy the requirements of retribution and deterrence, at the whole of the applicant's life. Fourteen years later, on 12 June 2008, Hardy's appeal for a review of his sentence was rejected. Mr Justice Teare, sitting at London's Royal Courts of Justice said:

> "In my judgment this is a case where the starting point under Schedule 21 [of the Criminal Justice Act 2003] is a whole life order on the grounds that this was a murder of three very young women involving sexual or sadistic conduct. Each murder was of a young girl. Two were found naked or almost naked and had a nipple removed. These matters indicate sexual or sadistic conduct. This conclusion is consistent with the view of the trial judge who considered the applicant to be 'utterly wicked'... Hardy 'does not accept his guilt and therefore shows no remorse,' however he is trusted to have access to sharp knives."

The judge concluded that: "this is a case where the gravity of the applicant's offences justifies a whole life order. Even if this were a case where a 30-year starting point was appropriate the aggravating features would mean that a whole life order would be the appropriate minimum period."

Becoming Unseen

Wilson *et al* (2010) considered why Hardy had become "unseen" and in doing so interviewed four journalists who worked on the case at the time of the murders. These four journalists either worked for the *Manchester Evening News* or for northern editions of national newspapers. All four suggested that the case should have been better known but, in considering why it had not, suggested four reasons. First, Hardy's murders had not been linked prior to going to trial and, specifically the police had suggested at the time that there was in fact no link between these crimes. This had meant that there was no "hunt" for a serial killer, which the press could report upon and which, in turn, would have generated more interest in the case. Second, they described a "North-South" divide between which "news" got reported, with events in the South being given greater prominence than stories generated in the North.

The final two reasons suggested by Wilson *et al's* interviewees were confusion as to whether or not Hardy was "mad or bad", the social status of the victims that he had killed and the areas of Manchester in which he had killed them. One of the journalists described the areas where these three victims had met their deaths as "low life" and another as "fish and chippy", all of which suggests that Hardy's victims were not considered as being "ideal victims" who would create sympathy with readers or viewers. Finally, the confusion as to whether Hardy was "mad or bad" was seen by all four journalists as a factor which had prevented him from being given a "catchy" nickname which would seemingly have allowed for greater reader, or viewer interest.

Prime Time?

The case of Trevor Hardy should have been "prime time", based on the news values that are identified by Jewkes. The fact that it was not suggests the need for further investigation into the interaction between serial killing and its representation in the media. Above all, what the Hardy case demonstrates are absences—absences in literature, absences in knowledge and in current academic theorising. In particular Hardy's case suggests that recent theorising about serial killers needs to consider why some killers remain in the public consciousness, while others—like Hardy—fade into obscurity.

Hardy's absence from the national media would also seem to challenge Jewkes's characterisation of the news values that structure newsworthiness, even if the values that she describes were specifically related to "a new millennium", and thus after Hardy started to kill. Nonetheless, what emerges from an analysis of the Hardy case is that the news agenda does not always conform to the criteria of newsworthiness that Jewkes and others have suggested might determine the level of interest in a case, and instead what has news value would seem to be more fluid, complex and, at times, baffling—even to those employed in the industry. In other words, real-life determinations of what is newsworthy can sometimes be governed by local and idiosyncratic factors, which do not necessarily fit neatly into any preconceived pattern of what events are seen to have news value. Journalists working in Manchester in the 1970s recognised the newsworthiness of the crimes that Hardy had committed, with one later describing it is as "ticking all the boxes" to have become a major story. Yet this was not reflected in the news coverage.

What emerges from the paucity of the news coverage about Hardy are a number of other issues which need to be considered when investigating the newsworthiness of any particular serial killing, and which can also be allied to suggestions of the importance of the "visual" as a key determinant of newsworthiness (see Greer, 2007, 2009). Indeed, there were no photographs of either Hardy or his female accomplice published at the time when the murders were being reported. The most salient of these other issues that should be considered is the time scale of when a number of murders are identified as being part of a series. In the Hardy case, the police—perhaps deliberately—ruled out any link between the murders of the second and third victims, at a time when the first victim was yet to be identified. One officer even told reporters that it "looks like a one off job". In all of this we can see an almost perfect example of the police acting in what Hall *et al* (1978: 58) have described as a "primary definer" of the news, and the media merely as a "secondary definer". As a result they simply reproduced an erroneous account from an expert and privileged source which served to down play the newsworthiness of Hardy's crimes. Moreover, by the time that the murders did come to be linked, the case had become *sub judice*, and strict reporting restrictions were implemented as Hardy had already been charged with the murders of Wanda Skala and Sharon Mosoph. Any careless reporting could be deemed to prejudice a jury and lead to the trial being ruled unsafe. Nor had there been a lengthy manhunt or press speculation, or police appeals for women to stay off the streets, all of which might have served to generate news coverage of the case. Indeed, by the time Hardy was caught the press could report very little, and so they were unable to create the "prime time" that Haggerty describes.

These processes which we have described would seem to be self-propelling. In other words, as soon as the public is informed, interest gathers and the story picks up pace. The more demand from the public, the more the story is reported, and so on. This is particularly apparent in an age where public interest can be easily monitored by viewing figures and website analysis. This propulsion is also fuelled by the allocation of media resources. Once news teams have been deployed they invariably file a story. All of this can be illustrated through the more recent example of serial killer Steve Wright, who murdered five women in Ipswich, Suffolk, in 2006. The Wright case generated more than six weeks of media frenzy, with the increasing number of victims leading to, for example, the costly deployment of news "anchors" to Ipswich. Once in place they were able to cover each twist and turn of the investigation with more gravitas than regular reporters in the field, which, in turn, appeared to generate more public attention. It was also apparent very quickly that the murders in Ipswich were linked. As such, it was safe to report that the police were hunting a serial killer, who, in turn, warned all women to stay indoors. Very quickly, the nation was gripped.

All of this is very different from the Hardy case, where the police denied any link until Hardy was charged with the crimes and, as a result, Hardy has been allowed to disappear into obscurity. How many other British serial killers have been similarly overlooked by privileging "expert" opinion from State sources? More broadly, how has our understanding of "violence" come to be viewed merely through the prism of certain types of interpersonal crimes, but largely ignores deaths caused by large corporations or indeed by the State itself? Indeed, in this specific case we might question why the media did not want to break the police's account of Hardy's murders and in doing so create a "moral panic" about his activities. That there was none might suggest that moral panics are reserved for specific cases within specific social settings, or as Hall has described it, only "tactically exploited" when the need arises.

As with any case study, it is, of course, difficult to generalise more broadly from the findings of one particular example. Indeed, as our brief discussion of the Wright case suggests, we do not seek to disagree more broadly from Haggerty's interesting provisional argument about the relationship between serial killing and modernity, and of the crucial role of the mass media within that relationship. However, what the Hardy case reveals is that this relationship might be more complex and is dependent on a range of case-specific variables that might, or might not, engender the circumstances which would allow any particular serial killer to have "newsworthiness" and thus become "prime time".

Revision

- Why does Haggerty suggest serial killers are "ready-made for prime time"?
- Describe how Jewkes characterises "news values"
- Who was Trevor Hardy?

- Account for the lack of media interest in Hardy's case, especially in comparison to the murders committed in 2006 by Steve Wright.

Further Reading

We mention a number of key books and articles within this chapter which should be consulted further. Chief amongst these are: K Haggerty (2009), 'Modern Serial Killers', *Crime, Media and Culture* 5(2): 168–87; Y Jewkes (2004), *Crime and Media*, London: Sage and D Wilson, H Tolputt, N Howe and D Kemp (2010), "When Serial Killers Go Unseen: The Case of Trevor Hardy," *Crime, Media and Culture* 6(2): 156–167. So as to get you to consider these issues more critically, we also mention G Slapper and D Tombs (1999), *Corporate Crime*, London: Longman; S Tombs and D Whyte (2007), *Safety Crimes*, Cullompton: Willan; and S Tombs and D Whyte (2008), *A Crisis of Enforcement: The Decriminalisation of Death and Injury at Work*, London: Centre for Crime and Justice Studies. For further reading about the media you should also consider consulting Steve Chibnall (1977), *Law and Order News*, London: Tavistock and Robert Reiner (2007), "Media-made Criminality: The Representation of Crime in the Mass Media", in M Maguire, R Morgan and R Reiner (eds.) (2012), *The Oxford Handbook of Criminology*, pp. 302–40, Oxford: Oxford University Press. Finally, it would be interesting to compare Hardy's case with that of the Ipswich serial killer Steve Wright. See, P Harrison and D Wilson (2007), *Hunting Evil: Inside the Ipswich Serial Killings*, London: Sphere.

CONCLUSION

This brief concluding chapter does not actually do what it "says on the tin". In other words, we offer no conclusion but instead briefly bring together a number of the threads that have guided the text. In doing so we ask that you reflect on some of the issues, themes and case studies which we have offered to you in the preceding chapters. Often these issues and themes were prompted by questions. These questions included:

- How should we define serial murder?;
- Who benefits from any particular definition adopted at particular times?;
- Why do people have such an interest in serial killers?; and
- How does the media shape our understanding of the phenomenon of serial murder?

In addition to these questions we also discussed the significance of gender in relation to those who become serial killers and how occupational choice might have helped to facilitate their murders. Case studies were offered to illustrate these ideas.

At a more theoretical level, we also questioned whether the medico-psychological or the structural tradition of analysing this phenomenon gave us greater insight and understanding about serial murder, and helped us to think about what we should do to lower the likelihood of serial murder from happening. Will "entering the mind" of a serial killer actually help to make our society safer, or are we better to concentrate on creating a society where the efforts of all are rewarded and the gap between the haves and the have-nots is reduced? Above all, we asked you to remain conscious of the people who fall victim to this appalling crime and what all of this might tell us about the type of society we have become.

Your answers to these questions and your acceptance of this type of reasoning are in the end the conclusion to this textbook.

INDEX

D

N

O

P

R

T

www.ingramcontent.com/pod-product-compliance
Lightning Source LLC
LaVergne TN
LVHW081934200926
848484LV00009B/2424